Get Serious!

A Survival Guide For Serious Catholics

By

Father James Farfaglia

~ 1 ~

ADDITIONAL PRAISE FOR *GET SERIOUS!*

If ever there was a time in the history of the Catholic Church when a small book like this one was needed, it is now. Father Farfaglia clears away all the cobwebs, the theological meanderings and the confusion by setting forth the truth – the nitty-gritty of what it means to be a serious Catholic and why it is the greatest blessing on earth to be in that number. I could write a lengthy commentary on all the reasons why I love this book and recommend it to every Catholic who needs to be inspired, affirmed or blessed, but let me just say this one little thing. Father has emphasized, over and over again, that we are first and foremost Christ's and He has got to be first in our life as well. There is no way around it and to accept this truth is to be filled with the very same love, hope and challenge that I think inspired Father to write this small volume. Soak it all in, read it more than once and praise God for Father James Farfaglia. Let us hope a whole lot of lukewarm Catholics join us because we serious Catholics shared a copy of it with them and that as a result, they too GET SERIOUS! – **Judie Brown, President of American Life League**

In a time when people are thirsting for straight talk Fr. Farfaglia gets right to the point. In no nonsense language, that especially young people are looking for, he gives a quick diagnosis and cure for the insanity of our times. For those who want to be a saint, or at least those who do not want to get lost, he points out a crystal clear path of sanity and peace that is simple: stop standing around and make a decision to allow your Catholic Faith to be the defining compass of your life. He even includes a step by step approach that would be great for youth groups, young adults, RCIA and other groups or individuals who are interested in growing in Christian maturity. May God bless Fr. Farfaglia's efforts to steer a confused generation to the Light of Jesus Christ. – **Fr. Sam Medley, SOLT**

DEDICATION

To all of the lay members of the Catholic Church throughout the world. The Second Vatican Council (1962 – 1965) reminded you that you are called to holiness, that you are to be active members of the Church and that you are to sanctify the temporal order.

If all of you were to seriously respond to this calling, the Church will be renewed and the world will be evangelized.

The sleeping giant must awaken.

"The Christian of tomorrow will be a mystic, one who has experienced something, or he will be nothing." – Karl Rahner

TABLE OF CONTENTS

FOREWORD

BY DEACON KEITH FOURNIER

With the issuance of a *motu proprio* on Tuesday, October 12, 2010, Pope Benedict XVI officially erected the new Pontifical Council for the New Evangelization. The action came through an Apostolic Letter entitled "Always and Everywhere". The title, as in all such letters, comes from the first line. "The Church has the duty to announce the Gospel of Jesus Christ always and everywhere."

This duty presupposes that we have encountered the One who is the source of this precious faith, Jesus Christ, and that our faith in Him is fully alive and mature. This is the task of the New Evangelization.

In this historic letter and act the Pope acknowledged the dire need of the Church for this New Evangelization and signals his commitment to leading us into a new missionary age. This action confirmed the heart of his pontificate and that of his beloved predecessor, the Venerable John Paul II.

This "New Evangelization" is intended for those in the Church who often do not understand the great gift given to them by the Lord when they were baptized into His Body. When they are awakened, formed in faith, and sent into a world which is desperately in need of the fullness of the Gospel as found within the full communion of the Catholic Church, this new missionary age will catch fire!

Father James Farfaglia just lit a match with this wonderful book entitled *"Get Serious! A Survival Guide for Serious Catholics"*.

It is an inspiring yet practical, catechetical yet simple, and substantive yet understandable manual for all Catholic Christians who want to grow in their faith by encountering the Lord in a continual relationship of conversion. These kinds of Catholics are the new missionaries whom the Lord is calling into the harvest at the beginning of the Third Millennium. They are the sleeping giant to whom Fr. James has dedicated this book.

I have stood at the intersection of faith and culture for decades, committed to this New Evangelization. It is an honor to stand with priests such as Father James Farfaglia. As the Editor in Chief of Catholic Online, it is a privilege to bring his homilies and writing to our global community.

When I was a child, my father used to sing an old song "Stouthearted men" whenever he was happy, filled with energy and inspired. Fr. James is a "stouthearted man", a "priest's priest". That is why I dubbed him the "Happy Priest" in his regular columns.

To this day, I recall the chorus of that song when I am challenged to act courageously in ministry. It describes Father James Farfaglia and the mission of this book:

"Give me some men who are stouthearted men, Who will fight, for the right they adore, Start me with ten who are stouthearted men, And I'll soon give you ten thousand more. Shoulder to shoulder and bolder and bolder, they grow as they go to the fore. Then there's nothing in the world can halt or mar a plan, When stout-hearted men can stick together man to man."

Of course, the appeal is to both men and women, in fact to all who hear the call of the Lord into this new missionary age. "*Get Serious! A Survival Guide for Serious Catholics*" will help you prepare for the work and reap the harvest. Read it and give it way to others, spread the flame!

~Deacon Keith Fournier is the editor-in-chief of Catholic Online, the largest Catholic website in the nation with over 120,000 daily readers. You can read his articles at <u>www.catholiconline.com</u>.

PREFACE

BY DONNA-MARIE COOPER O'BOYLE

Father James Farfaglia and I grew up together in the small rural town of Ridgefield, Connecticut. Well, kind of. You see, we both lived in Ridgefield and attended the same high school, but didn't know one another until many years later as Providence would have it.

Several years ago, I happened upon one of Father James's articles about the Catholic faith on a Catholic website, one that I wrote for as well. As I read to the bottom of what I thought was a great article, I noticed that he was raised in Ridgefield, Connecticut. Did I know him? I wondered. Did a classmate become a priest? I was curious. Then, I had to get in touch to find out. I called his rectory where he serves as pastor and that phone call actually began our friendship across the miles—he in Texas and me in Connecticut (still). We have since shared our faith through our writing, visits, retreats and friendship. I am blessed to know Father James and know you will be too, once you have read this book.

Knowing Father James Farfaglia as I do, I am not surprised that he decided to write this book *Get Serious! A Survival Guide for Serious Catholics.* In his own words, Father James tells us that, "this book is for serious Catholics or those who want to be serious in their relationship with God." If we are Catholic, it makes sense to me that we should want to get serious about our relationship with God. You've got the book in your hands to show you how.

Father James is a man who *seriously* lives his faith. At the same time, he doesn't wear blinders or hide away in the rectory. This priest is no stranger to the crazy culture in which we live in that can pull us away from the faith. His feet are no doubt firmly planted on the ground. Because he has seen it all, he is able to teach us through this book how to transcend the "insanity" around us and prayerfully remain sane, content and prayerful in our world today.

I think it's safe to say that Father James is more than a little fed up with the current state of affairs in our world and even in the Church; upset enough to not sit back and just moan about it, or worse yet, give up. Instead, this author took the time to craft a book in which he lovingly and practically gives us the tools to truly live the faith and carry out our duties as Catholics. He is both unabashed and passionate about getting us to understand the necessity of becoming *serious* about our faith and living it prayerfully. He encourages us to pray like we really mean it; like we are *serious* about really loving God. He tells us that, "the Catholic Church and the world need a big dosage of real, mature, authentic and coherent Christianity."

Whatever Father James does, he does with passion. I've seen him in action—whether it is administering the sacraments, getting after his congregation to get to Mass on time, sharing a meal with friends, or writing this book. He's not a gloom and doom kind of guy. Thank goodness! But, fortunately for us, he's an honest and compassionate priest, one who encourages the faithful not to become discouraged.

Thank God for Father James who admonishes us to wake up from our slumbers and embrace the faith and all it entails, so that we courageously pray for every gift that the Holy Spirit will bring to us, enabling us to become a radiant beacon of light to lead the way to Heaven for others.

Acknowledging that we live in a time of upheaval, Father James tells us that it's not unusual to feel overwhelmed or alarmed because of the upsetting things going on around us, including the clergy scandals, parishes shutting down, serious problems in our government as well as challenges and trouble at every turn. Because of these things, this no-nonsense author provides the tools to help us to not become victims or even despondent, but to instead become true disciples of Christ.

I love that throughout this book Father James allows us to peer into his own life. Sharing anecdotes, he ushers us into various chapters of his life—all in an effort to illustrate how we are to learn to pray and how we can deal with the difficulties that beset us.

No holds barred, Father James points out that "the narrow road to the Gospel is difficult to live. Nevertheless, it is the only road that leads to eternal life in heaven." He also openly warns us that without a serious prayer life we will be doomed. "Without daily contemplative prayer and daily Mass, or at least a prolonged visit before the Blessed Sacrament, you will be overpowered by anxiety and fear. You will implode without a personal relationship with God."

Father James shows us how to shape up our prayer lives, offering descriptions of several types of levels of prayer and specific prayers, as well as tips for a deeper prayer life. And more than that, Father James candidly acknowledges that, "prayer is a struggle," but it is "intertwined with blessings, moments of profound peace, and the obvious presence of God." Father James encourages the reader to find times of solitude to retreat to prayer and get closer to the "One who always seeks us and calls us to himself."

Jesus said, "Father, forgive them, for they do not know what they are doing." Reminding us that even in His suffering, Jesus loved from the Cross and continues to love us with a forgiving heart, Father James beckons us to do the same, to live holy lives and transcend the culture.

One Sunday, Father James preached in his homily, "In a world torn apart by war, violence, hatred, confusion and chaos, we all need to be ambassadors of God's love for humanity. We need to show the world that love is possible. We need to show the world that we believe in love! I would suffocate and die if I could not live each day in love. How absurd it is to be selfish. Only Jesus, the icon of the Father's love for you and me, shows us how to love. His way is simple, practical and clear. His way is spelled out for us in the New Testament. Love, love and love more and more each day. Stretch your heart and love more each day." And this is what Father James is all about—preaching what he lives, loving us enough to point us to our responsibilities as Catholics, striving to lead us all in the right direction and away from the corruption of the world, while teaching us all how to love.

There's much to be learned from this sincere and straightforward book. I'm reminded of something Saint Catherine of Siena said, which is: "When you are who you are called to be, you will set the world ablaze." Father James Farfaglia is an exemplary example of someone who unquestionably is living out who he is "called to be."

With Father James's guidance, let's pray that with God's infinite grace, together we can set the world ablaze!

~Donna-Marie Cooper O'Boyle, award-winning and best-selling Catholic author and EWTN TV host of "Everyday Blessings for Catholic Moms" can be reached at www.donnacooperoboyle.com

INTRODUCTION

If you want to spend most of eternity in purgatory or all of it in hell, this book is not for you. If you want to live an unhappy, lazy, complacent and meaningless life, this book is not for you either.

However, if you are a serious Catholic or you want to be serious in your relationship with God; if you really want to get to heaven; if you are sick and tired of the hypocrisy, corruption and insanity so characteristic of the times that we live in, then you need to read this book.

This book is a no-nonsense, practical approach to Catholicism and the spiritual life. Many books have been written about the spiritual life. All of them have their value and importance. However, this book deals with, in a very practical and up-front manner, the challenges that many Americans face who desire to lead a serious Catholic life. Use this book as a practical instructional manual.

I grew up in the small New England town of Ridgefield, Connecticut. My parents instilled in all of us very strong traditional and conservative values. I was very privileged to be a part of the founding class of Magdalen College which was founded in 1973. Magdalen College built upon what my parents gave me. My four years at Magdalen College were life changing and definitive. I am what I am today because of the formation that I received at Magdalen College. Through the prism of my four years at Magdalen College, I am offering to you a practical guide for personal happiness.

Caution: you are about to enter the "no whine zone."

CHAPTER ONE

HELLO...IS ANYBODY HOME?

Many years ago a very popular tune filled the radio airwaves. The song was from the 1966 Michael Caine movie called "Alfie."

"What's it all about, Alfie? Is it just for the moment we live? What's it all about when you sort it out, Alfie?"

Who am I? This is the most fundamental question that you need to ask yourself.

Most people wander through life like zombies. They do not even ask this question about themselves, nor are they even remotely interested. Their minds and consciences are numbed by blobbing out in front of the television every night after work for endless hours of mindless entertainment.

But if we take the time to ask ourselves, who am I, we are confronted with two realities; reality number one: there is a God. Number two: I am not him. I am a creature and I cannot be doing my own deal.

The insanity of our times is caused by the fact that most Americans are not listening. Most Americans are doing their own deal and most Americans have been spoiled rotten by an affluent society. Furthermore, most Americans live their lives without any reference to God the creator.

Why did God make me? God made me to know him, to love him, to serve him and to be happy with him in eternal life. Within these simple but profound words we find the purpose and meaning of our lives.

Before you can understand who you are as a Catholic, you need to understand who you are as a human being. You are not a monkey and you do not come from some blob of endless matter in the middle of outer space.

At one magical moment, a woman and a man joined together in the marital embrace of love. The woman is your mother and the man is your father. Within their ecstatic communion of love a new life began. That new life is you. God took the human elements provided by your mother and father, and gave you an immortal soul. At the moment of your conception you had all 46 chromosomes which made you a distinct, unrepeatable and a remarkable human being.

On the first day to the sixth day of your life, you moved from your mother's fallopian tube to her uterus which was, at that moment, the size of a pear. By the twenty-second day of your life, your heart began to beat with your own blood which was distinctly different from your mother's blood. By the end of the third week, your spinal column and nervous system were forming along with your liver, kidneys and intestines. By the fifth week your little eyes, legs and hands began to develop. By the sixth week, you had brain waves, a mouth, lips and fingernails. Your eyelids, toes and nose were present by the seventh week and you began to kick and swim around for the first time. Typically by this time your mother has just learned that she is pregnant with you.

By the eighth week, only two months of life, every one of your organs was in place. Your fingerprints began to form and you could even hear! You could even turn your head by the ninth and tenth weeks of life and even suck your thumb by the twelfth week.

Your heart pumped several quarts of blood through your little body every day by the fourteenth week. During your fourth month of life, you were about eight to ten inches long and you weighed about a half a pound. By the seventeenth week you were enjoying REM sleep.

And here is the best part of all; at twenty weeks old you began to recognize the greatest voice of all, your mom's.

Moving into the fifth and sixth months, your mother could feel you moving around and kicking her more and more. You grew to about twelve inches long and you weighed one and a half pounds.

During the last months inside your mother's womb you could open and close your eyes. You could see, hear, taste and touch. You could feel your mother's moods and you were by now pumping 300 gallons of blood per day.

And then came the great moment, nine months after the miracle of your life began, when you wanted to come out and see your mom and dad for the first time.

So, now that you know who you are as an amazing human being, who are you as a Catholic?

The Catholic Church is comprised of three categories of people: the laity, the clergy and the religious.

All of us start out as being part of the laity. All of the laity begin to live out their Catholic life within the lay single state. Most lay single people are called to the vocation of holy matrimony. Some of the laity are called by God to be members of the clergy and the religious. These are the bishops, priests, deacons, sisters and brothers.

Let us zero in on the laity. Who are you in the Church of God?

First of all, no matter how spiritual you may be, you are not a part of the clergy or the religious. This means that you should not be walking around with rosary beads hanging from your eyeballs. You are in the world. You go to school. You go to work. You do your food shopping and you eat at restaurants. You can't look like some kind of a weirdo or a religious fanatic. If you want to bring people to the Gospel of Jesus Christ, you need to look normal and professional.

As a lay person, your mom and dad asked your parish priest to baptize you soon after you were born. When your priest poured the waters of baptism over your little head and said, "I baptize you, in the name of the Father, and of the Son, and of the Holy Spirit," you became a member of what Saint Peter calls "the common priesthood of the faithful" (1 Peter 2: 9-10).

As a member of the common priesthood of the faithful, you have certain rights and duties. Within these rights and duties, you have two fundamental tasks.

First of all, you are called by God to be holy. Everyone has the possibility of becoming a saint. This does not mean that you are going to have beams of light shooting out from your forehead.

Holiness means that you are going to live in union with God through prayer and the seven sacraments. It means that the Gospel of Jesus Christ is going to be your way of living out your life within the circumstances of your daily life.

Secondly, your task is to sanctify what the Church calls "the temporal order." The "temporal order" is everything outside of your parish campus. As soon as you leave Mass and pull out into the street, you are in the temporal order.

Your home, your neighborhood, your place of work, your school, the supermarket, the restaurant, the ball field and the movie theatre are all part of the temporal order.

You sanctify the temporal order by the way you live out your Christian way of life. However, not only are you to be a witness, you are also called to be active in the vineyard of the Lord. You have limitless possibilities of spreading the Gospel. You have countless opportunities to bring many people to God.

As the pastor of a new parish, I am very blessed to be surrounded by many parishioners who take their lay vocation seriously. Their commitment to the lay apostolate is inspiring and it allows me to be an effective pastor of a growing Catholic community.

From 1962-1965 all of the Catholic Bishops of the entire world got together with Pope John XXIII and then with Pope Paul VI for a very important meeting in Rome.

This meeting, the Second Vatican Council, reminded you that you are called to holiness and to the apostolate. Some years after the conclusion of Vatican II, three laymen heard the call of the Catholic Church. They clearly saw the needs of our times and decided to use the gifts that God had given them by founding a new institution of higher learning.

In 1973, three friends decided to start a Catholic college. Peter Sampo was a college professor, John Meehan was a high school teacher and Francis Boucher was a business man. They were concerned about all of the insanity around them and they felt the need to do something about it. So, they decided to start a small liberal-arts Catholic college.

With lots of faith and very little money they cut a deal with the owner of the Bedford Motel in Bedford, New Hampshire and the motel became Magdalen College.

Little by little, concerned parents started to hear about the new endeavor. One evening after dinner, my mother was sitting in the kitchen sipping her coffee while reading the evening newspaper. "Jim, look at this." She was referring to a tiny article carried by the Associated Press about a new Catholic college that was beginning in New Hampshire.

I had already been accepted by two colleges where I was set on studying political science and I was not concerned about my mother's sudden excitement.

Another mother saw the same article and invited Peter Sampo and Francis Boucher, who were travelling the New York area, to meet with parents who were concerned about what was going on in the Catholic Church and the country.

My Dad attended the Thursday evening meeting. He was impressed and invited Sampo and Boucher over to the house the following Saturday evening for wine and cheese. We had a very enjoyable visit and the two founders invited me to visit the "college."

My parents and I visited and the rest is history.

At Magdalen College we were immersed in the writings of Plato, Aristotle, Augustine, Thomas Aquinas and the other great thinkers of western civilization. Our professors made their writings come alive. The fundamental question "who am I?" is a question that the ancient philosophers explored. Throughout my college years this question was posed, challenging us to ask ourselves the same thing.

I am very grateful that these three men started a new college, because it is there that I found out who I am and what I am supposed to be doing in the Church of God.

Armed with a clear understanding of your identity, you can begin to be who you are supposed to be and to understand what you are supposed to do. You can't begin to develop a serious spiritual life until you first figure out who you really are in the Catholic Church.

Suggested Reading

The Dogmatic Constitution on the Church (*Lumen Gentium*) – especially Chapter Four - The Second Vatican Council

The Decree on the Apostolate of Lay People (*Apostolicam acuositatem*) - The Second Vatican Council

Apostolic Exhortation, *Christefidelis Laici* - John Paul II

CHAPTER TWO

THE FIRST STEP TOWARDS A NEW YOU

For the first time in my life I was away from the supervision of my parents. I had to wake up in the morning, make my bed, clean my room, polish my shoes, be punctual for classes and do my homework without my Mom or Dad saying anything if I was off the mark.

This was college and I began a very exciting adventure in September, 1974 at 18 years of age. Without really knowing what I was getting into, my college was concerned about the intricate details of discipline.

October, 1974 was our first Parents' Weekend. Keep in mind that Magdalen College had just opened its doors in September and I was a member of the first group of freshmen students. For my roommate and I, this was our first test in self-discipline. James Hickel, from Anchorage, Alaska and I failed miserably.

When my parents entered our room, my Mom was shocked. Magdalen College is in New Hampshire and our floor was covered with about two inches of dead leaves. Mom immediately got out the vacuum cleaner, but she should have used a rake.

Jim and I finished our first semester well, but we were certainly not working to our potential. John Meehan, one of the founders of the college and the dean of students, knew that.

We both went home for our first Christmas vacation. When we returned to school for our second semester, Meehan came into our room and sat us both down. His attitude was like that of a Marine drill sergeant biting the heads off of a couple of new recruits.

"You goofballs are wasting your time and money," he shouted with his characteristic Boston accent.

Meehan knew our potential and he believed that any of his students could do great things. So, he proceeded to give us a simple tool to achieve new and promising goals. "You dopes need a schedule. You lazy slobs need to form your will. Stop fiddilin' and didilin' and do something with your lives. It is time to stop picking your nose and get your butt into gear."

Wow! Instinctively we both knew that Meehan was right and we enthusiastically accepted his challenge.

Jim and I sat down in front of my typewriter (these were the days before laptops) and we proceeded to develop a schedule for every day of the week and every minute of each day.

We decided to begin every day at 5 AM rather than the usual rolling into breakfast with toothpicks holding up our eyelids (Meehan's proverbial phrase when his students were falling asleep in class).

Hickel was athletic and I was not. So, upon his suggestion we decided to hop out of bed and go for a mile run every morning no matter what the weather was like (remember, we are still in New Hampshire and the winters are freezing).

I can recall coming back from a run with ice in my nose.

The running thing was not enough. We took freezing cold showers every morning in order to "beat the flesh" and then we sat down and studied for an hour before breakfast the one subject that we hated the most – Latin.

Jim and I were not the brightest bulbs in the box, but at the end of the semester, our grades were among the best. Everyone knew that we were on to something.

Discipline is essential. You will not be able to live out a serious spiritual life without it.

The most vital aspect of self-discipline is acquiring personal organization. That's right. You need to get out of lapland (another well-known term used by Meehan) and develop your own personal schedule.

Sit down and write out your schedule and stick to it. If you are single, find a friend who will hold you accountable. If you are married, make a schedule for the entire family. Work together with your spouse and your children as you help each other fulfill your daily schedule. Be accountable to each other.

When Jim and I wrote out our first schedule, we put our signature on the bottom of the page. We both signed it as if we were signing it with our own blood.

Both you and your children need to acquire the basic aspects of human formation. Clean rooms, well groomed hair, ironed clothes, polished shoes and personal hygiene all make up the fundamentals of what it means to be truly human.

Grace does not work without human nature, it builds upon it. First a man, first a woman, and then the saint.

Developing a family schedule will allow you to pray together as a family. Why not run your family like a domestic monastery? Ring a bell to let everyone know that it is time for breakfast, homework, rosary or a family outing. Remember, mom is not a short-order cook and the kitchen has to close at some moment in the day.

Homeschooling families have a privileged opportunity to make their homes into a true sanctuary of order. You can create your own schedule rather than be led by the schedule of a school.

Create a realistic family schedule. With infants and small children you will have to develop something appropriate to their ages. Print out your schedule and post it on a bulletin board where everyone can see it. Plug in Catholic feast days, national holidays, vacations, visits to your parents, the kids activities and the activities of your parish family.

It is important that your children get to bed early. After a long day, you and your spouse need quiet time together.

When I was a little kid, there were many summer nights when I used to wonder why we were in bed while it was still light outside and our little friends were still playing out in the street. Years later, my mother confessed to us that when she had had enough, she used to push the arm on the kitchen clock an hour ahead so that we would all think that it was time to turn in.

Be sure to schedule in a "date night" with your spouse. This should take place once a week or every other week depending on your family circumstances. Have a quiet dinner together, alone. Go for a walk, alone. Plan weekend get-aways, alone. Plan an annual vacation, alone. Time away together, as a couple, without the children, is an important means to keep your relationship fresh.

John Meehan's lively invitation to get on a schedule was a turning point in my life. My decision was a major step in the process that made me the man and the priest that I am today. My first experience of a daily schedule formed my will, allowed me to use my time well and gave me freedom because I was no longer wasting large amounts of time.

For those of you who are married, it is very important that you keep it real simple. Your kids do not have to be involved in multiple sports nor do they need   to play numerous musical instruments. One sport and one musical instrument is enough.

Honestly, in my view, organized sports, as they are understood today, are huge distractions from family life. They form a trap that only breaks down the family. I think that it is ludicrous to be travelling all over the state and even all over the country for a child's game. Whatever happened to kids just being kids? Whatever happened to kids playing in neighborhoods?

Mothers with children at home need to stay home and take care of them. Families with stay-home moms function much better. The home needs to be the priority. Not only do young children need a mother to be home, but high school kids need their mom as well.

A husband needs to be proactive, industrious, diligent and responsible by providing for the family without leaning on his wife financially. Too many mothers work all day only to come home to situations where they are expected to do everything. This causes the wife to lose respect for her husband and to lose patience with her children.

Moreover, not only is it essential to organize your time, it is also necessary to discipline the use of your income. Create a budget and stick to it. Live within your means and avoid unnecessary credit card debt. Financial discipline is critical to family life. If you commit to staying home with your children, be assured that God will provide.

Besides, you might find that it is cheaper for mom to stay home with the kids rather than go to work.

This of course, is not to take away from amazing women who out of necessity may have to work in order that their families can survive. Computers allow women to create home-based businesses if extra-income is needed.

Over the years I have seen many hard working and creative parishioners find practical solutions that have worked well for their families. Here are just a few examples.

Rhonda and Oscar built a new home a few years ago. Near the entrance of their beautiful residence they built a room where Rhonda can run her nails business while the kids are in school.

Rosie, a hard working Mexican immigrant who became an American citizen not too long ago, worked as my bookkeeper a few hours each day. We worked out her schedule in such a way that she could pick up her three boys from school. When they did not have school, they studied and played in an adjoining office. During the day her little new-born rested in a cradle near her work station. Rosie, however, realized that it was time to stay home. So she diligently helped me in training a new bookkeeper. Although I miss working with her, she made the correct decision to focus on her family.

Still another example of ways women can add to the family income is Kateri, who met her husband Joe while going to college in Corpus Christi. They have three young children whom they homeschool. Kateri has built a reputation as one of the best photographers in the city. She is a stay-home mom. However, on Saturdays, she brings extra income into the house by doing weddings. Joe arranges his work schedule so that he can spend the day with his boys.

Discipline and order are key components for a successful spiritual life. "You dopes need a schedule. You lazy slobs need to form your will. Stop fiddilin' and didilin' and do something with your lives. It is time to stop picking your nose and get your butt into gear."

What is your decision?

Suggested Resources

The 7 Habits of Highly Effective People – Stephen R. Covey

The 7 Habits of Highly Effective Families – Stephen R. Covey

First Things First – Stephen R. Covey

Time Management for Catholics – Dave Durand

A Mother's Rule of Life – Holly Pierlot

The Heart of Motherhood – Donna-Marie Cooper O'Boyle

The Domestic Church: Room by Room a Mother's Study Guide – Donna-Marie Cooper O'Boyle

Total Money Makeover – Dave Ramsey

CHAPTER THREE

DEVELOPING A SPIRITUAL LIFE

If you have decided to read this chapter, I am assuming that you have made the choice to change your life. Happiness and success in this life are only possible with a serious relationship with God. The duties of family life, work and school take up most of the hours of each day. Therefore, a well organized and realistic schedule of your time is necessary in order to have the quiet moments that you need in order to develop a serious spiritual life.

I am very happy when I find individuals who choose to get out of their spiritual kindergarten and decide to advance to a much deeper relationship with God. I honestly do not understand people who willfully exist in the shallowness of complacency and immaturity.

In order to survive the turbulent and uncertain times that we live in, a consistent spiritual life is necessary. The lazy and the apathetic will remain in the halls of the walking dead.

At Magdalen College prayer was taken very seriously. We were expected to attend Mass every

Sunday and we had some kind of formal prayer time in the chapel throughout the week.

During my years at the college we had Scripture reading every Monday, Tuesday and Thursday. We had Mass on Wednesdays and Rosary on Fridays. Chapel time took place just before lunch. The idea of having formal prayer time for a bunch of Catholic "pagans" was an excellent initiative. It disposed and opened the soul for more.

Our first chaplain was an elderly priest by the name of Fr. Rodolphe Drapeau. Father Drapeau was a retired priest from the diocese of Manchester, New Hampshire. He had heard about the new college from Francis Boucher, one of the founders of Magdalen College, and he wanted to help. He made himself available for Mass and confessions on Wednesdays and Sundays.

Father was tough as nails, but when you got to know him, he was very kind and understanding. It always seemed that he was hollering at you in the confessional. He was not being mean; he was simply old and hard of hearing. In order to avoid hearing what was being said by him to others who were in the confessional, we usually had to run out of the chapel because he was talking so loud.

Fr. Drapeau was the best priest that had come into my life since my boyhood pastor, Msgr. James McLaughlin, who was transferred from my parish around 1968. Father's homilies were clear, to the point and demanding. In the confessional he was the same way and he really challenged all of us to live a true Catholic life.

My Mom and Dad pray the Rosary every day. However, growing up, we were not really into the Rosary. Nevertheless, Sunday Mass and frequent confession were as basic to us as having dinner every night as a family. As parents, you never know when your children will really catch on to the fundamentals of the Catholic Faith. The fruits that you are seeking may take decades to be revealed to you. Be patient and trust God. But, remain diligent and persevere.

As founding members of a new college, our class had many unique opportunities to start things up. Aside from founding the Magdalen College social club where I ran a Saturday night film series, for some reason it occurred to me to begin an evening Rosary at 8:30 PM. The Rosary took place every night, except for Fridays, since we already had the Rosary in the morning.

The idea of beginning an evening Rosary for the student body came to me before I even thought about the possibility of becoming a priest. However, as my spiritual life began to really take off, it was during one of those evening Rosaries that my journey to the Catholic priesthood began.

One evening in the early part of my sophomore year, after the evening Rosary, I felt a profound urge to stay in the chapel and pray. Everyone left to go and study or socialize, and I was left alone with Jesus. There were no visions, no voices, but the presence of Jesus was so intimate and awesome. I looked at the tabernacle and I said, "I know that you want something big from me. I don't know what it is. Just tell me and I will do it."

Thirty minutes later I returned to my room. It just so happened that the next day was a Wednesday. I was the altar server that morning. At the moment of the consecration when Father Drapeau elevated the Host, I could feel this tremendous urge that said, *"you have to do what he is doing."* The outpouring of grace was so powerful that it almost caused me to lose my balance as I was kneeling on the side of the altar.

When I left the chapel, there was no doubt in my mind that God wanted me to be a priest. Initially there was fear; most especially, the fear of more studies. Studies did not come easy to me. It was always a lot of work. Shortly after these experiences, during that same school year, the freshmen were assigned to give a talk on a saint of their choice for All Saints Day.

During the special activity where each freshman got up and gave their little talk, one girl gave a short talk on the life of Saint John Vianney. I had never heard of the Curé of Ars. She spoke about his difficulty with studies and how he persevered to become a great priest and a great saint. When she finished, I said to myself: "If he can do it, so can I." My fears were gone. After graduating college, I went to the seminary. They were years filled with profound happiness and excitement. I was ordained on December 24, 1987, in Rome.

At Magdalen College I began to understand that prayer is not just asking God for something. *"In your prayers do not babble as the pagans do, for they think that by using many words they will make themselves heard. Do not be like them; your Father knows what you need before you ask him"* (Matthew 6: 7-8). Now I have come to realize that prayer is being in love with the God of unconditional love.

I would like you to discover what I have discovered.

Remember, Jesus wants us to have life. He wants us to be happy. He wants us to have the best possible life here on earth. He wants to fill us with his divine life, sanctifying grace, so that we may enter into his joy. He wants us to experience his peace. He wants us to be with him in eternal life in heaven. He only wants the best for us. This is why he wants us to open our hearts to him and let him enter in. *"I have come so that they may have life and have it to the full"* (John 10: 10).

Have no fear of allowing Jesus to enter into your life. Do not fear the most exciting, most joyful and the most powerful relationship known to the human person.

"So often today man does not know what is within him, in the depths of his mind and heart. So often he is uncertain about the meaning of his life on this earth. He is assailed by doubt, a doubt which turns into despair. We ask you therefore, we beg you with humility and trust, let Christ speak to man. He alone has words of life, yes, of eternal life" (Pope John Paul II, homily, October 22, 1978).

We are made by God to live forever. We have been given the gift of an immortal soul. *"For God formed man to be imperishable; the image of his own nature he made him"* (Wisdom 2: 23).

Jesus does not want us to live a life of sadness. He does not want us to wallow in doubt, frustration and uncertainty. He wants us to live. By embracing God's will and by carrying our cross with patience, joy and love, we can find deep happiness even in the midst of profound suffering. He takes the hand of Jairus' daughter and says *"Talitha koum, which means little girl, I say to you, arise!"* (Mark 5: 41). The Lord takes each of us by the hand and tells us to arise. Arise from your darkness. Arise from your doubt. Arise from your despair. Arise from your pain. Arise from your sin. Arise and live!

"Ask, and it will be given to you; seek and you will find; knock, and it will be open to you. For every one who asks receives, and he who seeks finds, and to him who knocks it will be opened" (Luke 11: 15).

Nevertheless, it is true that prayer is not an easy enterprise. The spiritual life will always be a battle. There always will be obstacles that are necessary to overcome if we wish to live a life of prayer.

First of all, many people struggle with distractions when they pray. I have always encouraged people to be patient when they are distracted. However, it is true that distractions are rather normal, especially for all those who are beginning to develop a prayer life.

Personal discipline, choosing a suitable place, using a good text when necessary and selecting a proper time for prayer are all important aspects when determined to overcome distractions in prayer.

Secondly, aridity is another major obstacle that people struggle to overcome. However, it must be understood that spiritual dryness is a normal road of purification that the Lord uses in order to bring us to greater heights of the spiritual life.

The quality of prayer must not be measured by personal feelings. Feelings come and go. Our personal experience of God through prayer will fill us with peace and provide renewal and strength, but it is important that we leave consolations to the will of God.

Thirdly, many people become impatient with God because they want instant answers. God is not a computer. Our God is a loving Father who knows all of our needs.

Finally, probably the biggest obstacle is that most people are just too busy. Too many people are like Martha, *"anxious and worried about many things"* (Luke 10: 41). Too many people have fallen into the terrible trap of what I call the idolatry of work, thus making their work a complete obsession to the detriment of their families and personal health. Most Americans live in order to work rather than work in order to live. Man was not made for work; work was made for man.

We might ask ourselves when was the last time that we stopped to watch the sunrise or the sunset? Can we recall walking on the beach, enjoying the fragrance of a beautiful flower, cherishing the innocent smile of a child or gazing at the moon and the night sky filled with stars?

Again we might ask ourselves when was the last time that we enjoyed dinner with family and friends, or turned off our cell phone and refrained from checking our email at every moment? Excessive work and travel, excessive involvement in sports and entertainment are tearing us apart. Is it really necessary to be travelling long distances for your kids sporting events?

The Apostles asked Jesus to teach them how to pray. They witnessed firsthand how Jesus prayed. The Gospels narrate how Jesus would spend entire nights in prayer. Many times the Evangelists point to the eyes of Jesus and how he would look up to heaven before pronouncing a teaching. They longed to pray like the Master. In response to their quest, Jesus taught them the most perfect prayer.

The Lord's Prayer contains every petition that we need for our earthly existence and our eternal salvation. It is precisely with the very words that Jesus taught us, that we can find deep consolation and strength during the many trials and tribulations of our journey towards eternal life in heaven.

Prayer is a struggle. The struggle is intertwined with blessings, moments of profound peace and the obvious presence of God. Trust and perseverance: two lessons that we are reminded of as we read over the gospels.

In order that we may experience God in our daily lives we need to pray every day. Mother Theresa once said: "We need to find God and God cannot be found in noise and restlessness. God is the friend of silence. See how nature--trees and flowers and grass--grow in silence. See the stars, the moon and the sun, how they move in silence. The more we receive in silent prayer, the more we can give in our active life."

But, in order to pray, we need to obtain the ability to be alone with ourselves. It is difficult to be alone in contemporary society. Even when we are alone, the noise of our own worries and fears drown out the silence of God's voice. Many people are incapable of being alone and they immediately feel an obsession to talk with someone on a cell phone or fool around with email.

We all need moments of solitude. Spending a quiet time before the Eucharist; reading the Scriptures during a peaceful moment at home; taking tranquil walks through the woods or along the beach, are necessary activities for our soul. In order to be with God, we must develop the ability to be alone with ourselves.

Silence will deepen any relationship. Silence allows us to listen and to gaze. Let us take the time to be silent so that we can grow in our relationship with the One who always seeks us and calls us to himself.

What then should your daily prayer life look like? More than likely, your life is very busy and you do not have a whole lot of time for prayer. However, I would like to offer you three levels of a daily prayer routine for the busy layperson in the modern world. Please do not make any excuses. I have seen very busy executives live the kind of prayer life that I am urging you to implement into your daily schedule.

Level One

Morning Prayer from the Liturgy of the Hours or the monthly magazine "The Magnificat"

15 minutes of meditation – use a small text from the Bible, or a chapter from *My Daily Bread* or *The Imitation of Christ*

Daily Rosary

Night Prayer from the Liturgy of the Hours or "The Magnificat" with a brief examination of conscience

Sunday Mass

Monthly Confession and whenever necessary

Level Two

Morning Prayer from the Liturgy of the Hours or the monthly magazine "The Magnificat"

15 minutes of meditation – use a small text from the Bible, or a chapter from *My Daily Bread* or *The Imitation of Christ*

Daily Rosary

Night Prayer from the Liturgy of the Hours or "The Magnificat" with a brief examination of conscience

Daily Mass

Monthly Confession and whenever necessary

Annual Retreat

Level Three

Morning Prayer from the Liturgy of the Hours or the monthly magazine "The Magnificat"

30 minutes of meditation – use a small text from the Bible, or a chapter from *My Daily Bread* or *The Imitation of Christ*

Daily Rosary

Night Prayer from the Liturgy of the Hours or "The Magnificat" with a brief examination of conscience

Daily Mass

Monthly Confession and whenever necessary

Annual Retreat

Prayer is not always easy. There will be moments when you simply do not feel like praying. You will battle with distractions and moments of dryness. Do not worry. Welcome to the human race. Stick to your prayer schedule. Persevere and leave the rest to the Holy Spirit.

At one moment during my third year at Magdalen College, John Meehan must have noticed that my personal prayer life was developing rather nicely. One evening outside of the chapel he said to me, "If you don't pray, you will be a lousy priest. If you don't pray, I will have nothing to do with you."

Since Magdalen College, prayer has been the rock solid foundation that has sustained my vocation throughout all of these many years. Once in a while a thought about slacking off from prayer might occur to me. However, immediately the voice of the drill sergeant pulls me out of lapland and it brings me back to reality.

I honestly do not know what it takes for people to really want to pray. Perhaps spiritual thirst is a gift. However, we need to remember the words of Sacred Scripture. *"The nearer you go to God, the nearer he will come to you"* (James 4:8). Persist on praying no matter what. Persevere in your daily prayer routine and let the Holy Spirit take it from there. If you feel that your faith is weak, ask the Holy Spirit to deepen your faith. *"Ask, and it will be given to you; search, and you will find; knock, and the door will be opened to you. For the one who asks always receives; the one who searches always finds; the one who knocks will always have the door opened to him"* (Matthew 7: 7-8).

When I speak about the importance of developing a consistent prayer life, I am speaking about formal moments of prayer inserted throughout your daily schedule. Linked to these formal moments of prayer is the interior life. The interior life consists of sporadic moments of prayer throughout the day and the cultivation of interior silence as you carry out the demands of your busy life.

By offering your day to God each day through the Morning Offering prayer or in your own words, your whole day becomes your prayer to God. Every good act of your day becomes an offering to God. Moreover, by offering your day for a particular intention or a number of intentions, each one of your acts becomes a powerful tool for the salvation of souls. When you look at your day through the eyes of faith, your work, the duties of your state in life, your moments of relaxation and even your sleep becomes a prayer.

When you reach the second and third levels of the spiritual life, you may feel the need for guidance from a spiritual director. A spiritual director is a qualified person who can help you on your journey. A good spiritual director is a beautiful gift from God and not an easy person to find. The priest that you go to confession to and your spiritual director may be two different people, or your confessor can also be your spiritual director. This is a personal decision. However, given the fact that qualified spiritual directors are hard to come by, be grateful if you can find a holy priest who can be your confessor on a regular basis. Within the Sacrament of Confession you can ask him for advice and counsel whenever they are needed.

The gospels continually display a two-sided equation: man's search for God and God's search for man.

In the gospel narrative about the Samaritan woman, we are struck by the fact that Jesus is tired and he stops at the well to rest. The heat is oppressive and Jesus is exhausted. Nevertheless, forgetful of his own personal needs, Jesus is absorbed by an uncontainable desire for the eternal salvation of the Samaritan woman.

This uncontainable desire for the eternal salvation of all mankind is illustrated in the beautiful words that Our Lord spoke to St. Margaret Mary during the third apparition of his Sacred Heart, which took place on June 16, 1675: "Behold the Heart which has so loved men that it has spared nothing, even to exhausting and consuming itself, in order to testify its love; and in return, I receive from the greater part only ingratitude, by their irreverence and sacrilege, and by the coldness and contempt they have for me in this sacrament of love".

Just as Jesus sought the eternal salvation of the Samaritan woman, he seeks us out as well. He continually reaches out to us and desires our eternal salvation.

A number of years ago I asked a friend what was objectively keeping him from going to Mass every day. "Nothing," he honestly said. Since then, this very busy and successful business man attends Mass every day.

Basic Prayers

The Lord's Prayer
Our Father, Who art in heaven,
Hallowed be Thy Name.
Thy Kingdom come.
Thy Will be done, on earth as it is in Heaven. Give us this day our daily bread.
And forgive us our trespasses,
as we forgive those who trespass against us.
And lead us not into temptation,
but deliver us from evil. Amen.

The Hail Mary
Hail Mary,
Full of Grace,
The Lord is with thee.
Blessed art thou among women,
and blessed is the fruit
of thy womb, Jesus.
Holy Mary,
Mother of God,
pray for us sinners now,
and at the hour of death. Amen.

The Glory Be
Glory be to the Father,
and to the Son,
and to the Holy Spirit.
As it was in the beginning,
is now,
and ever shall be,
world without end. Amen.

The Morning Offering
O Jesus, through the Immaculate Heart of Mary,
I offer you my prayers, works, joys and sufferings
of this day for all the intentions
of your Sacred Heart, in union with the Holy
Sacrifice of the Mass throughout the world, in
thanksgiving for your favors, in reparation for my
sins, for the intentions of all my relatives and

friends and in particular for the intentions of the
Holy Father. Amen.

The Act of Contrition
O my God,
I am heartily sorry for
having offended thee,
and I detest all my sins,
because I dread the loss of heaven,
and the pains of hell;
but most of all because
they offend thee, my God,
Who art all good and
deserving of all my love.
I firmly resolve,
with the help of thy grace,
to confess my sins,
to do penance,
and to amend my life. Amen.

The Apostles Creed
I believe in God, the Father Almighty, creator of
heaven and earth;
and in Jesus Christ, his only Son Our Lord,
Who was conceived by the Holy Spirit, born of the
Virgin Mary, suffered under Pontius Pilate, was
crucified, died, and was buried.
He descended into Hell; the third day he rose again
from the dead;

He ascended into heaven, and sitteth at the right hand of God, the Father almighty; from thence he shall come to judge the living and the dead.
I believe in the Holy Spirit, the holy Catholic Church, the communion of saints, the forgiveness of sins, the resurrection of the body and life everlasting.
Amen.

Prayer to St. Michael the Archangel
St. Michael the Archangel,
defend us in battle.
Be our defense against the wickedness and snares of the devil.
May God rebuke him, we humbly pray,
and do thou,
O prince of the heavenly hosts,
by the power of God,
thrust into hell Satan,
and all the evil spirits,
who prowl about the world
seeking the ruin of souls. Amen.

The Memorare
Remember, O most gracious Virgin Mary, that never was it known that anyone who fled to thy protection, implored thy help, or sought thine intercession was left unaided. Inspired by this confidence, I fly unto thee, O Virgin of virgins, my

mother; to thee do I come, before thee I stand, sinful and sorrowful. O Mother of the Word Incarnate, despise not my petitions, but in thy mercy hear and answer me. Amen.

The Angelus
The Angel of the Lord declared to Mary:
And she conceived of the Holy Spirit.

Hail Mary…

Behold the handmaid of the Lord: Be it done unto me according to thy word.

Hail Mary . . .

And the Word was made Flesh: And dwelt among us.

Hail Mary . . .

Pray for us, O Holy Mother of God, that we may be made worthy of the promises of Christ.

Let us pray:

Pour forth, we beseech thee, O Lord, thy grace into our hearts; that we, to whom the incarnation of Christ, thy Son, was made known by the message of an angel, may by his passion and Cross be brought to the glory of his resurrection, through the same Christ Our Lord. Amen.

Regina Coeli (prayed during the Easter Season in place of the Angelus)
Queen of Heaven, rejoice, alleluia.
 For he whom you did merit to bear, alleluia.

Has risen, as he said, alleluia.
Pray for us to God, alleluia.

Rejoice and be glad, O Virgin Mary, alleluia.
For the Lord has truly risen, alleluia.

Let us pray. O God, who gave joy to the world through the resurrection of thy Son, our Lord Jesus Christ, grant we beseech Thee, that through the intercession of the Virgin Mary, His Mother, we may obtain the joys of everlasting life. Through the same Christ our Lord. Amen.

Act of Faith
O my God, I firmly believe that you are one God in three divine persons, Father, Son and Holy Spirit. I believe that your divine Son became man and died for our sins, and that he will come to judge the living and the dead. I believe these and all the truths

which the holy Catholic Church teaches, because in revealing them you can neither deceive nor be deceived.

Act of Hope

O my God, relying on your almighty power and infinite mercy and promises, I hope to obtain pardon of my sins, the help of your grace and life everlasting, through the merits of Jesus Christ, my Lord and Redeemer. Amen.

Act of Love

O my God, I love you above all things, with my whole heart and soul, because you are all-good and worthy of all love. I love my neighbor as myself for the love of you. I forgive all who have injured me, and I ask pardon of all whom I have injured.

Prayer to the Holy Spirit

Come Holy Spirit, fill the hearts of your faithful and kindle in them the fire of your love.

V. Send forth your Spirit and they shall be created.

R. And you shall renew the face of the earth.

Let us pray.

O, God, who by the light of the Holy Spirit, did instruct the hearts of the faithful, grant that by the same Holy Spirit we may be truly wise and ever enjoy his consolations. Through Christ Our Lord. Amen.

How to pray the Rosary

1. Make the Sign of the Cross and say the Apostles' Creed.

2. Say the Our Father.

3. Say three Hail Marys.

4. Say the Glory be to the Father.

5. Announce the first mystery; then say the Our Father.

6. Say ten Hail Marys, while meditating on the mystery.

7. Say the Glory be to the Father.

   Announce the second mystery; then say the Our Father. Repeat 6 and 7 and continue with the third, fourth and fifth mysteries in the same manner.

After each decade say the following prayer requested by the Blessed Virgin Mary at Fatima: "O my Jesus, forgive us our sins, save us from the fires of hell, lead all souls to heaven, especially those who have most need of your mercy."

.

After the Rosary:

Hail, Holy Queen, Mother of Mercy, our life, our sweetness and our hope! To thee do we cry, poor banished children of Eve; to thee do we send up our sighs, mourning and weeping in this valley of tears. Turn then, most gracious advocate, thine eyes of mercy toward us, and after this our exile, show unto us the blessed fruit of thy womb, Jesus. O clement, O loving, O sweet Virgin Mary!

> V. Pray for us, O Holy Mother of God.
> R. That we may be made worthy of the promises of Christ.

Let us pray. O God, whose only begotten Son, by his life, death and resurrection, has purchased for us the rewards of eternal life, grant, we beseech thee, that meditating upon these mysteries of the Most Holy Rosary of the Blessed Virgin Mary, we may imitate what they contain and obtain what they promise, through the same Christ Our Lord. Amen.

The Mysteries of the Rosary

Glorious Mysteries - the Resurrection, the Ascension, the Descent of the Holy Spirit, the Assumption of Mary, the Crowning of Mary

Joyful Mysteries – the Annunciation, the Visitation, the Birth of Jesus, the Presentation of Jesus in the Temple, the Finding of Jesus in the Temple

Sorrowful Mysteries – the Agony in the Garden, the Scourging at the Pillar, the Crowning with thorns, the Carrying of the Cross, the Crucifixion

Luminous Mysteries – the Baptism of Jesus in the Jordan, the Wedding at Cana, the Proclamation of the Kingdom, the Transfiguration, the Institution of the Eucharist

As suggested by the Pope John Paul II the Joyful mysteries are said on Monday and Saturday, the Luminous on Thursday, the Sorrowful on Tuesday and Friday, and the Glorious on Wednesday and Sunday (with this exception: Sundays of Christmas season - The Joyful; Sundays of Lent - Sorrowful).

How to meditate

1. Select a short text to meditate on. Suggestions include selections from the Holy Bible or spiritual books such as *My Daily Bread* and *The Imitation of Christ.*

2. Begin the meditation by making acts of faith, hope and love by using the prayers that are listed above or in your own words such as "Jesus I believe in you. Jesus I trust you. Jesus I love you." Pray briefly to the Holy Spirit and ask Mary, the Mother of Jesus, to assist you in this time of prayer. Offer this time of prayer for a particular intention.

3. Slowly read the text. Reflect on the meaning of the text and how it applies to your life. What is God asking of you in light of this text? What virtue or virtues do you need to practice in your daily life? If you are meditating on the Scriptures, you can also place yourself within the scene of the gospel passage. For example, if you are meditating on the birth or the passion of Jesus, using your imagination put yourself into the scene. What do you see? What do you hear?

4. Speak to Jesus and Mary. Tell them how much you love them. Ask them to give you

the strength to carry your cross and to love even more.

5. Thank the Holy Spirit and Mary for this time of prayer.
6. Make a concrete and practical resolution for the day.

How to get into contemplative prayer

Once you acquire the habit of meditating every day, you may have a thirst to go even deeper by substituting meditation with contemplative prayer. Contemplative prayer is an advanced way of praying. This way of praying should be the goal of your prayer life. Be patient and consistent. By forming firm prayer habits, you will grow.

"Contemplation is a *gaze* of faith, fixed on Jesus" (Catechism of the Catholic Church, #2715). Contemplation is the prayer of the heart and not of the mind. It does not use a text and may use a word or a phrase as a way of entering into the prayer of silence and faith. Contemplative prayer may focus on a word or one may simply *be* in the presence of God. It is the prayer of the listening heart. The goal of contemplative prayer is to enter into the presence of God where there are no words, concepts or images. It is the prayer of being in love. It is important to remember that contemplative prayer is a gift of the Holy Spirit. The method that follows is not contemplative prayer in and of itself. The method helps to predispose us for the reception of the gift.

Before the Blessed Sacrament - sit or kneel. Gaze into the Tabernacle or look into the Monstrance. Be still. Focus on your breathing. Ask Mary to help you to pray. Pray to the Holy Spirit. Then peacefully repeat a word or a phrase: Jesus; Jesus I love you; Jesus I trust in you; Father; Father, into your hands I commend my spirit, etc. Do not continue to repeat the word or the words over and over again. Only use the word or the phrase when your mind begins to wander. The purpose of using a word is to express your intention of being in the presence of God. Focus your gaze on the Eucharist. Be open to whatever Jesus is asking of you. Don't be looking for messages. Just be with God.

At home - sit or kneel. Close your eyes. Again, be still and focus on your breathing. Ask Mary to help you to pray. Pray to the Holy Spirit. As before, repeat a word or a phrase. Do not repeat the word or words over and over again. Remember to use the word only when your mind begins to wander. The purpose of the word is to express your intention to be in the presence of God. Focus your gaze on the loving presence of God within you. If you begin to feel embraced by God, be still and be silent. Just allow the Holy Spirit to pray within you.

Suggested Reading

The Spiritual Journey - Francis Kelly Nemeck, OMI

Contemplation - Francis Kelly Nemeck, OMI

Fire Within – Thomas Dubay, S.M.

Intimacy with God - Thomas Keating, O.C.S.O.

Being in Love - William Johnston, S.J.

The Inner Eye of Love – William Johnston, S.J.

Silent Music – William Johnston, S.J.

The Mysticism of the Cloud of Unknowing – William Johnston, S.J.

When The Well Runs Dry – Thomas H. Green, S.J.

Centering Prayer and the Healing of the Unconscious - Fr. Murchadh O' Madagáin

Sensing Your Hidden Presence – Ignacio Larrañaga, O.F.M.CAP.

CHAPTER FOUR

BLESS ME FATHER FOR I HAVE SINNED

Before John Meehan challenged Jim Hickel and me to establish a daily schedule, he challenged our entire class with an excellent explanation of the Sacrament of Confession. Aside from being the Dean of Students, Meehan was our philosophy and theology professor.

It was December, 1974 and we were about to leave for our first Christmas vacation. John invited us to a special talk that he gave to us one Thursday afternoon outside of our regular class schedule.

Meehan proceeded to give us a basic and clear explanation about mortal sin, venial sin and how to make a good confession. He urged us to make a general confession of our entire past life and that a young priest would be waiting for us at the local parish. Strategically he had already asked the recently ordained Father George Ham who at that time was the Assistant at Saint Elizabeth Ann Seaton Parish in Bedford, to sit in the confessional that evening and wait for us to arrive.

We all accepted Meehan's invitation.

When it was my turn to enter into the darkened confessional, I went through my well prepared list. Father Ham encouraged me with the utmost kindness. As Father prayed the words of absolution, I experienced a profound peace and happiness that are impossible to describe in words.

Upon leaving the confessional my eyes were fixed upon the large and beautiful stained glass window located above one of the side doors of the church. I felt as if I was going to fly through the window. The weight of caked-on sin was gone and I experienced for the first time in my adult life the freedom of the children of God. *"When Christ freed us, he meant us to remain free. Stand firm, therefore, and do not submit again to the yoke of slavery"* (Galatians: 5:1).

That moment at Saint Elizabeth Ann Seton parish was the most crucial moment in my life. This was the moment when I began an adult relationship with the Lord and a real struggle with myself.

We are all sinners. I am a sinner and you are a sinner. We sin every day. We have to take sin very seriously. *"If we say we have no sin in us, we are deceiving ourselves and refusing to admit to the truth; but if we acknowledge our sins, then God who is faithful and just will forgive our sins and purify us from everything that is wrong. To say that we have never sinned is to call God a liar and to show that his word is not in us"* (1John 1: 8-10).

What is sin? The Catechism of the Catholic Church gives us a concise definition. "Sin is an offense against reason, truth and right conscience; it is failure in genuine love for God and neighbor caused by a perverse attachment to certain goods. It wounds the nature of man and injures human solidarity. It has been defined as an utterance, a deed, or a desire contrary to the eternal law" (#1849).

Scripture tells us that actual sin is divided into two classifications: mortal sin and venial sin. *"There is a sin that leads to death..."* (1John 5:16). *"Every kind of wickedness is sin, but not all sin leads to death"* (1John 5:17).

Mortal sin is forgiven through the Sacrament of Confession. The Catechism of the Catholic Church teaches: "Confession to a priest is an essential part of the Sacrament of Penance. All mortal sins of which penitents after a diligent self-examination are conscious must be recounted by them in confession..." (#1456).

We all take as a given that the goal of Christianity is to enter into eternal life; however, attaining this goal requires intense daily effort on our part. The spiritual life is not an easy endeavor because of our wounded human nature. True, Baptism washes away Original Sin, but we are left with the effects of Original Sin. We do not have complete control over ourselves. The spiritual life is a continual battle.

As a result of Original Sin, our weakened wills, darkened intellects and inflamed passions will always move us in the wrong direction. Continual effort is necessary to control the inner movement of our ego and allow the presence of grace to take control of our thoughts, desires and actions. The battle of the spiritual life might be compared to walking in a river against the current. If we do not continue walking or reaching out toward a rock for support, then the current will most assuredly carry us in the opposite direction.

The Catechism tells us, "Because man is a composite being, spirit and body, there already exists a certain tension in him; a certain struggle of tendencies between spirit and flesh develops. But in fact this struggle belongs to the heritage of sin. It is a consequence of sin and at the same time a confirmation of it. It is part of the daily experience of the spiritual battle" (#2516).

If the spiritual life is a continual struggle because of Original Sin, the present circumstances of our contemporary culture make this struggle even more difficult. We have all grown up in a culture that denies us nothing. Everything is permissible. We tend to view discipline, self-control and virtue with distaste. The producers and writers of television programs, films, music and other aspects of pop culture know exactly what buttons to push to gently ease us into accepting a more permissive attitude toward interests and activities that we ought to shun. Our decadent world is thus made more attractive to our fallen human nature. We find it easier and easier to succumb to any of the seven deadly sins.

Just like all the other sacraments of the Church, Jesus instituted the Sacrament of Confession. The Church has always understood the Scriptural reference for the Sacrament of Confession to be John 20: 22-23: *"Receive the Holy Spirit. For those whose sins you forgive, they are forgiven; for those whose sins you retain, they are retained."*

What an immense gift we have been given! The Sacrament of Confession is an enormous source of interior peace. The priest raises his hand, and then with a blessing pronounces those amazing words: I absolve you from your sins. At that moment, we know that God has heard our cry for forgiveness, and we have been pardoned of our sins. *"God, who is rich in mercy..."* (Ephesians 2: 4).

For me, Confession has been, along with the Eucharist, my greatest source of strength and peace during my journey with the Lord Jesus. As a parish priest, my greatest joys are celebrating the Eucharist for my people and hearing confessions. I am overjoyed when people use the Sacrament of Confession on a regular basis. My best parishioners are those who are going to Confession on a regular basis because these are the people who are in the battle. They are alive, not dead like complacent, unresponsive zombies. My heaviest cross as a priest has been the rejection of Confession by many people. If they only knew what would give them such peace and happiness. I do not worry about the people who are going to Confession. I worry about those who never go.

The Parable of the Prodigal Son is by far one of the most beautiful narratives of the Holy Bible and it will help us understand the Sacrament of Confession.

Let us take a moment and read the complete narrative from the Gospel of Saint Luke.

"A man had two sons, and the younger son said to his father, 'Father, give me the share of your estate that should come to me.' So the father divided the property between them. After a few days, the younger son collected all his belongings and set off to a distant country where he squandered his inheritance on a life of dissipation.

When he had freely spent everything, a severe famine struck that country, and he found himself in dire need. So he hired himself out to one of the local citizens who sent him to his farm to tend the swine. And he longed to eat his fill of the pods on which the swine fed, but nobody gave him any.

Coming to his senses he thought, 'How many of my father's hired workers have more than enough food to eat, but here am I, dying from hunger. I shall get up and go to my father and I shall say to him, 'Father, I have sinned against heaven and against you. I no longer deserve to be called your son; treat me as you would treat one of your hired workers.'

So he got up and went back to his father. While he was still a long way off, his father caught sight of him, and was filled with compassion. He ran to his son, embraced him and kissed him. His son said to him, 'Father, I have sinned against heaven and against you; I no longer deserve to be called your son.'

But his father ordered his servants, 'Quickly bring the finest robe and put it on him; put a ring on his finger and sandals on his feet. Take the fattened calf and slaughter it. Then let us celebrate with a feast, because this son of mine was dead, and has come to life again; he was lost, and has been found.' Then the celebration began.

Now the older son had been out in the field and, on his way back, as he neared the house, he heard the sound of music and dancing. He called one of the servants and asked what this might mean. The servant said to him, 'Your brother has returned and your father has slaughtered the fattened calf because he has him back safe and sound.'

He became angry, and when he refused to enter the house, his father came out and pleaded with him. He said to his father in reply, 'Look, all these years I served you and not once did I disobey your orders; yet you never gave me even a young goat to feast on with my friends. But when your son returns who swallowed up your property with prostitutes, for him you slaughter the fattened calf.'

He said to him, 'My son, you are here with me always; everything I have is yours. But now we must celebrate and rejoice, because your brother was dead and has come to life again; he was lost and has been found'" (Luke 15: 11-32).

The conduct of the father in the parable reveals to us the love and mercy of God. The father not only welcomes his prodigal son, but also celebrates his return with immense joy.

The prodigal son's decision to leave his father's house and to immerse himself into a life of rebellion, clearly illustrates the nature of sin. Every sin is an abuse of human freedom. When we sin, we defy God who loves us unconditionally. The consequences of sin are always disastrous.

The hunger that the prodigal son experiences parallels the anxiety and emptiness that we feel when we are far from God due to sin. We can never be ourselves when we sin. Sin will always bring us to our lowest state and cause us to even become perverted if we were ever to persist in a life of sinfulness.

The prodigal son experiences the profound sadness that sin causes. He turns away from his attachments to the things of this world and looks within himself. His introspection allows him to make a vital decision: *"I shall get up and go to my father..."* (Luke 15: 18).

Like the father of the parable, God is always waiting for our return. We are filled with profound emotion as God always runs to us in order to forgive, heal and sustain us. As we experience the embrace of the unconditional love of God, we cry out with immense joy and gratitude: Abba, Father!

The robe, ring, sandals and the celebration are all symbols that Jesus brilliantly uses to explain the reality of our union with God through sanctifying grace. Sin is the separation from the father's house.

Adam and Eve realized that they were naked when they had sinned. Joseph's coat was removed when he was sold into slavery. The wedding guest in the gospel parable of the wedding feast was expelled from the wedding feast because *"he was not wearing a wedding garment"* (Matthew 22: 11). The prodigal son was dressed with the finest robe when he was restored to his father's house.

Biblically, a ring is always a symbol of union, covenant, love and commitment. Just as marriage joins a man and a woman, and they become one, sanctifying grace joins us to God and we become one with him. The Catechism of the Catholic Church says: "Grace is a participation in the life of God. It introduces us into the intimacy of the Trinitarian life. By baptism the Christian participates in the grace of Christ, the Head of his Body. As an adopted son he can henceforth call God 'Father,' in union with the only Son. He receives the life of the Spirit who breathes clarity into him and who forms the Church" (#1997).

During the time of Jesus, slaves and servants never wore footwear. Their relationship was essentially different to the household that they served. Only members of the family wore sandals. The prodigal son is given sandals because through his conversion, he is no longer a slave to sin.

The celebration takes place because of the immense joy that the father experiences due to the return of his son. At the same time, our union with God is the only source of true and lasting joy. Augustine famously wrote: "You called, you shouted, and you broke through my deafness. You flashed, you shone, and you dispelled my blindness. You breathed your fragrance on me; I drew in breath and now I pant for you. I have tasted you, now I hunger and thirst for more. You touched me, and I burned for your peace" (Confessions, Book 7).

What can we say about the older brother? His response to the father's mercy indicates that his years of obedience have been years of duty and not filial service. Perhaps he was simply going through the motions, remaining at home simply to enjoy the benefits of a comfortable life.

Like the Pharisees, he is self-righteous, incapable of love and therefore, incapable of forgiving anyone. His mind is dark and calculating. It is possible that his anger is rooted in the fact that he too would like to leave the father's house and live a life of sin. His life may be pure and noble, but his heart is attached to things that he would like to do, but avoids them because of his vanity and superiority complex.

God's love is far greater than man's capacity to love. God can forgive what man refuses to forgive. The love, mercy and compassion of God can overcome the rebellion of the human heart. Nevertheless, there are many who refuse his love and prefer to live far from the father's house.

God patiently seeks the conversion of every person. God will do everything that he can do to save us. We are objects of God's infinite love and can personally experience his love. However, God's infinite wisdom respects our freedom. We can accept or reject God's invitation to experience eternal joy and peace.

It is through the Sacrament of Confession that we experience true joy and peace. God restores our dignity and our freedom and we experience his unconditional love. As we humbly kneel and recognize our sin, God celebrates our repentance and dresses us with the finest robe, a beautiful ring and lovely sandals.

Let us take a close look as to how we make a good confession.

First and foremost you have to form your conscience. We hear a lot about following our conscience. Yes, we do have to follow our conscience, but our conscience must be informed and well formed. If we do not take the time to develop an informed and well formed conscience, an erroneous conscience will shipwreck our journey to eternal life.

Our conscience must be formed by objective truth. Basically this means that the 10 Commandments, the New Testament and the Magisterium of the Catholic Church comprise our road map to holiness, interior peace and eternal salvation.

We inform and form our conscience by knowing what the Ten Commandments demand from us. We live out the objective moral law by being imbued with the entire message of the Gospel. We need to study and assimilate the teachings of the Catholic Church. This means that we have to read.

If you can figure out who is playing on Monday night football, you can figure out what God expects of you. The truth is not complicated. In fact Jesus tells us, *"You shall know the truth and the truth shall make you free"* (John 8: 32).

Unlike the complicated discourse of many philosophers and religious leaders, Our Lord's teaching is simple and easy enough for everyone to understand. The message is so clear and precise that his words are irresistible to all those who listen.

Who is this man that has divided history into two parts? Who is this man that has divided nations? Who is this man for whom many of his followers have given their lives rather than deny him?

John the Baptist knew him immediately, *"Behold, the Lamb of God, who takes away the sin of the world. Now I have seen and testified that he is the Son of God"* (John 1: 29; 34).

What do we need to do in order to truly know Christ Jesus? Above all, we must be open. Far too many people attempt to live Christianity based upon their own terms. They do not come to the Lord with open minds and hearts. Far too many remove pages from the Scriptures and reduce Christianity to their own comfort level. When we are completely open, the Holy Spirit floods our souls with his loving and peaceful presence. He will not enter locked doors and windows that we have shut. God respects our freedom.

Only the open can believe and see.

Knowledge automatically brings us to love. We only love that which we know. Our love for the Lord must be authentic and real. Hypocrisy repulsed the Lord. *"In the written scroll it is prescribed for me, to do your will, O my God, is my delight, and your law is within my heart"* (Psalm 40: 8).

Love brings about transformation. The goal of discipleship is to die to self so that the Lord may live within us. Whether that disciple is Paul, Sosthenes, John the Baptist, or everyone *who has called upon the name of our Lord Jesus Christ,* (1Corinthians 1: 2) every true disciple is sanctified and made holy by the Lord who is the *light to the nations* (Isaiah 49: 6).

At our own Baptism, the priest touched our ears and said *Ephphetha, be open.* There is something about the modern world that is preventing us from listening to God. Some even listen, only to reject what they hear.

The narrow road of the Gospel is difficult to live. The grace of God makes Christianity not only possible; it is the only road that leads to eternal life in heaven.

So, getting back to the Sacrament of Confession, please keep in mind that it is very easy to go to Confession. Here is a very simple and basic rundown of the steps for a good confession.

FIGURE OUT WHAT YOU NEED TO TELL THE PRIEST

Examine your conscience and plan out your confession before going into the confessional. It is not a bad idea to write out your confession. Some people keep spiritual journals in order to track their spiritual progress. If you have any mortal sins, it is necessary to tell them to the priest. Do not get into details. Just tell the priest your sins and how many times they occurred. Then, proceed to tell him your venial sins. It may not always be possible to remember every venial sin. Focus on the venial sins that occur most often. If you do not have any mortal sins, the frequent confession of venial sins is very healthy for spiritual progress. Confession is not only for the forgiveness of mortal sin. The Sacrament of Reconciliation increases sanctifying grace and it allows us to know ourselves better. Sanctifying grace is a participation in God's inner life. We are elevated and transformed through this gift that we received at our Baptism.

We should go to Confession every month. Although venial sins are forgiven by the reception of Holy Communion or an Act of Contrition, confessing our venial sins and imperfections is an excellent tool for spiritual progress. The first goal of our spiritual journey is to eliminate mortal sin from our lives. The second goal is to continue chipping away at our venial sins.

The Sacrament Confession not only forgives sin. Through this sacrament, God purifies our soul from the people, places and things that we are attached to that cause us to sin. The Sacrament of Confession also fills us with an increase in the gifts of faith, hope, charity and fortitude. It provides us with a deeper knowledge of ourselves, it provides us with the graces that we need to avoid future sin and it brings about in us to a deeper intimacy with God.

If you are dealing with mortal sin, do not sleep in mortal sin. Find a good priest and go to Confession immediately. Especially when dealing with sexual sin, it is very important to be very demanding on yourself. It is possible to live habitually in the state of grace. Again, this is the first goal of the spiritual life – to live in the state of grace, free from mortal sin.

Mortal sin occurs when there is full knowledge that something is a sin; when there is full consent and when the act is grave or serious. A venial sin occurs when there is full knowledge that something is a sin; when there is full consent, but the act is less grave or serious. Temptation is not a sin. There is no need to mention temptations or struggles within the Sacrament of Confession.

Here is a simple guide that will help you examine your conscience. The list that is provided does not contain every sin, but the list does contain the most common sins that people struggle with.

Most common mortal sins (any of these sins need to be confessed to a priest within the Sacrament of Confession before receiving Holy Communion)

Superstitious practices such as the use of the Ouija board, tarot cards, the crystal ball, the egg and horoscopes

Taking the Lord's name in vain

Purposely missing Mass on Sunday and Holy Days of Obligation

Serious acts of disobedience against parents; serious rebellion against the Magisterium of the Church

Abortion, euthanasia, in-vitro fertilization, contraception, sterilization, masturbation, pre-marital sex, viewing pornography, giving into impure thoughts and desires

Marriage after divorce without an annulment

Serious lies

Serious acts of stealing, serious acts of injustice such as an employer not giving a proper wage to workers

Serious acts of anger, hatred, slander and calumny

Most common venial sins (confession of these sins is not necessary before receiving Holy Communion, but monthly confession is recommended for our spiritual progress as we strive to eliminate our venial sins)

Smaller acts of disobedience to parents

Impatience and anger

Selfishness

Vanity, jealousy and envy

Laziness

Small lies

Stealing something small

Sins of omission

WHAT TO DO INSIDE THE CONFESSIONAL

Once you are inside the confessional start with the sign of the cross and say, "Bless me Father for I have sinned. It has been _____ since my last confession." Telling the priest how long it has been since your last confession is an important help for the priest. If your last confession was a month or two ago, that tells the priest that you are probably going to confession on a regular basis and that you are seriously working on your spiritual life. If it has been a long time since your last confession, the priest may help you make a good confession. If you are going to confession a lot, it may indicate that you are struggling with a particular sin and the priest can give you concrete advice as to how to overcome the sin that you are dealing with. Confessions that are close together may also indicate that you are looking for sin where there is no sin. This is called scrupulosity. It is not necessary to go to confession to the same priest, but it is very good practice. A regular confessor can help you form and inform your conscience well.

Tell the priest your sins. Just say your sins. Listen to the advice that the priest gives to you. The priest is not there to yell at you. If he is a good priest, he will give you good advice. Usually I encourage my penitents to begin again with deep interior peace. Sometimes I will ask them how their prayer life is going. There are other times when I will gently suggest ways to overcome the sins that they are struggling with.

Remember, a priest can never tell anyone what you have spoken to him about within the Sacrament of Confession. The *seal* of the Sacrament of Confession is very serious and a priest can never say anything to anyone, even in order to protect his own life or reputation. Whatever you say in the confessional stays in the confessional.

The priest then absolves you from your sins by saying: "God, the Father of mercies, through the death and resurrection of his Son has reconciled the world to himself and sent the Holy Spirit among us for the forgiveness of sins; through the ministry of the Church may God give you pardon and peace, and I absolve you from you sins in the name of the Father, and of the Son and of the Holy Spirit. Amen."

If there is a long line of people waiting for Confession, the priest may use a shorter version by saying, "I absolve you from your sins in the name of the Father, and of the Son and of the Holy Spirit. Amen." This is perfectly valid as well.

After the priest pronounces the prayer of absolution, he then gives you a penance to do. A penance is an act by which we make up, in some way, for the sins that we have committed. Sometimes the penance may be something that you pray inside the church when your confession is finished, or the penance might be some act that you do when you go home. The priest may tell you to say the Act of Contrition inside the confessional or inside the church. Either way is perfectly fine.

It is essential that you always remember never to repeat to your confessor a sin, no matter how embarrassing that sin may have been, ever again. It is over because it is over. A sin that you have confessed to a priest is forgiven by God forever. God can forgive anyone of anything. Forgive yourself and keep moving forward. Discouragement is a huge obstacle in the spiritual life.

The Sacrament of Confession is your best weapon in your fight against sin and spiritual tepidity. The Sacrament of Confession is the first act of the Risen Lord. On Easter Sunday Jesus gave the Church the authority to forgive sins. *"Receive the Holy Spirit. For those whose sins you forgive, they are forgiven; for those whose sins you retain, they are retained"* (John 20: 22-23).

Applied to our practical daily living, the reality of the Risen Jesus and the Sacrament of Confession fill us with profound peace. There is no need to worry or to fear. He is truly with us. With Jesus, we know that we are journeying, not to the sunset, but to the sunrise. We enter into a new relationship with God when we really believe that God is as Jesus told us that he is. We become absolutely sure of his love. We become absolutely convinced that he is above all else a redeeming God. The fear of suffering and death vanishes, for suffering and death means going to the one God who is the awesome God of love. In reality, our life long journey is a journey to the eternal Easter in heaven.

When we truly believe, we enter into a new relationship with life itself. When we make Jesus our way of life, life becomes new. Life is clad with a new loveliness, a new light and a new strength. When we embrace Jesus as our Lord and Savior, when we develop a personal relationship with him, we realize that life does not end, it changes and it goes from incompletion to completion, from imperfection to perfection, from time to eternity.

When we truly believe in Jesus, we are resurrected in this life because we are freed from the fear and worry that are characteristic of a godless life; we are freed from the unhappiness of a life filled with sin; we are freed from the loneliness of a life without meaning. When we walk with Jesus and follow his way, life becomes so powerful that it cannot die but must find in death the transition to a higher life.

The bodily resurrection of Jesus from the dead makes our entire journey to eternal life tangible, real, certain, and credible. Because Jesus is physically alive, his Church is visible. Because Jesus is corporeal, the sacraments are visible aqueducts of his divine life. Because Jesus physically transcends time and space, he remains with us in the Eucharist as the "medicine of immortality" (cf. Catechism of the Catholic Church, #1405). Because Jesus has truly risen from the dead and ascended to the Father, we await with joyful hope his return in glory.

SEXUAL SIN IS THE BATTLE OF OUR TIMES

We are constantly bombarded with immoral sexual images and the time has come for all of us to make radical decisions. Uncontrolled and unmonitored use of the television and the Internet *are* occasions of sin. Technology gives you many opportunities to control what you watch on television and how you use the Internet. Pornography is a terrible addiction. Cut the cable and rent movies from Netflix. Through Netflix you can control what you watch. If you are addicted to Internet pornography, maybe it would be better not to have a computer at home.

Contraception, in all of its forms, is rooted in the sins of lust and selfishness. Contraception foments lust and selfishness. Chuck the condoms and the pills in the garbage. If your priest is telling you that contraception is permissible, it is time to look for another parish. If you had a tubal ligation or a vasectomy, almost all acts of sterilization can be reversed, even tubals. But the issue with vasectomies is that a reversal five or more years after the fact, though technically possible, is not likely to be fruitful in terms of conceptions, due to the immune system's reactions against the sperm. With tubals, the issue is purely a technical one, but through specialists and modern techniques, almost all can be reversed. However, in some cases, risks maybe involved in doing a reversal, therefore people are not morally obligated to have a reversal in order to be reconciled through the Sacrament of Confession. Pastorally, I recommend that everyone who has been sterilized and is still within child-bearing age should consult with a Catholic doctor who is faithful to the Magisterium of the Church regarding the possibility of a reversal.

Back in 1968 Pope Paul VI warned the world what would happen if contraception were to be made available: "Let them first consider how easily this course of action could open wide the way for marital infidelity and a general lowering of moral standards. Not much experience is needed to be fully aware of human weakness and to understand that human beings—and especially the young, who are so exposed to temptation—need incentives to keep the moral law, and it is an evil thing to make it easy for them to break that law. Another effect that gives cause for alarm is that a man who grows accustomed to the use of contraceptive methods may forget the reverence due to a woman, and, disregarding her physical and emotional equilibrium, reduce her to being a mere instrument for the satisfaction of his own desires, no longer considering her as his partner whom he should surround with care and affection" (Pope Paul VI, *Humanae Vitae*, 17).

When it comes to sexuality, we have to be very demanding with ourselves.

Remember that the Catechism of the Catholic Church calls self-mastery a training in human freedom. "The alternative is clear: either man governs his passions and finds peace, or he lets himself be dominated by them and becomes unhappy" (#2339). The Catechism goes on to say that "self-mastery is a long and exacting work. One can never consider it acquired once and for all. It presupposes renewed effort at all stages of life" (#2342).

It is quite possible that when we consider the demands of our spiritual life and the impact on us of the continuous bombardment we receive from the prevailing culture, we may simply throw up our hands in despair and give in. Without a doubt, authentic Christianity is difficult to live and demands radical decisions on our part. We must never be afraid of the struggle. Remember, Babe Ruth struck out 1,330 times, but he also hit 714 home runs.

Although developing and strengthening our spiritual life requires an intense effort on our part, all our efforts will only be successful with the help of God's grace. A daily disciplined regimen of prayer, scripture reading and sacramental life helps to develop those channels of grace through which the Holy Spirit gives us the ability to control ourselves and conquer our baser tendencies.

Since the spiritual life is a daily struggle, we must understand that there are always risks involved. Thus we sin, failing once again through human weakness or a lack of ardent love. But the true disciple of Jesus will always get up and begin again. This is why the Sacrament of Confession is so crucial for perseverance in our journey towards eternal life.

Sin will always be a continual struggle. Sexual sins are not the only sins that we deal with. However, chastity is certainly the struggle of our times. After more than twenty-two years as a priest, I am convinced that the capital sin of lust is not the only reason why serious Catholics continually struggle with sexual sin.

I believe, that for the serious disciple of Christ, the cause of continual sexual sin is compounded by an epidemic disorder in our emotions.

Dr. Conrad W. Baars, M.D. called it an emotional deprivation disorder. Mother Theresa called it the famine of love. The on-going struggle with masturbation, pornography and fornication is rooted in the fact that modern man feels unloved, isolated and alone.

I believe that this emotional disorder is caused by the following factors:

1. The unborn child that was unwanted and unloved by his or her mother;
2. The infant that was not breastfed when it was possible to do so;
3. The infant that was left in day care;
4. Mothers who work outside of the home;
5. Fathers who have abandoned their families;
6. The infant and the child that is not held enough by mother and father
7. The infant and the child that was sexually and/or psychologically abused
8. Children of alcoholic parent(s)
9. Children of a parent or parents who are addicted to drugs
10. Children of divorced parents

After reading this list, you can see that most of us have been damaged by a very dysfunctional society. What then is the solution for this serious problem?

Traditional Catholic spirituality has always placed great importance on mortification to control and integrate our sexual desires. Mortification is an act of abnegation or self-denial. Mortification implies detachment and renunciation. It also implies the continual struggle against the evil tendencies of fallen human nature in an effort to curb and eliminate their influence.

Without a doubt, concupiscence will always be something that we will have to deal with until the resurrection of the body. However, based on long pastoral experience, because of the pathology of the emotional disorder that we are all dealing with, it is of great importance that we focus our attention on how to love correctly and how to existentially experience that love within our emotional world.

Christopher West, writing on his website says, "It is precisely this liberation that allows us to discover what John Paul II called 'mature purity.' In mature purity 'man enjoys the fruits of victory over concupiscence' (TOB 58:7). This victory is gradual and certainly remains fragile here on earth, but it is nonetheless real. For those graced with its fruits, a whole new world opens up - another way of seeing, thinking, living, talking, loving, praying. But to those who cannot imagine freedom from concupiscence, such a way of seeing, living, talking, loving, and praying not only seems unusual

- but improper, imprudent, dangerous, or even perverse" (www.christopherwest.com).

Action points for emotional healing are:

1. Develop and maintain the prayer life that I already have spoken to you about. You need to experience God's awesome love for you on an emotional level.
2. Connect with your family. If your family is dysfunctional find someone in your family that you can connect with. The experience of some kind of connection with your family or a family member is very important. There may be some sad situations where this may be impossible, but for most people, they can at least connect with one or a few family members.
3. Have good, solid friendships. You do not need to have many friends; you need at least one true friend. The Bible calls one true friend a real treasure.
4. Be an active member of your parish. Being part of a church family is very important for a healthy emotional life.
5. Enjoy life and laugh a lot.

6. Learn how to forgive everyone of everything and leave your troubles at the foot of the Cross.

I am totally convinced that if you put these action points into practice, joined together with a serious life of mortification, the struggle with sexual sin will diminish or disappear all together. Your sexuality can be transformed by Jesus. You can live with interior peace and freedom. But all of this will take continual hard work and vigilance. Remember, the Catholic Faith is not for wimps.

As a final consideration, maybe you have asked yourself why is it necessary to confess your sins to a Catholic priest? Blessed John Henry Newman, who was beatified by Pope Benedict XVI on September 19, 2010, provides us with a beautiful answer.

"And yet, my brethren, so it is, he has sent forth for the ministry of reconciliation, not Angels, but men; he has sent forth your brethren to you, not beings of some unknown nature and some strange blood, but of your own bone and your own flesh, to preach to you. 'Ye men of Galilee, why stand ye gazing up into heaven?' Here is the royal style and tone in which Angels speak to men, even though these men be Apostles; it is the tone of those who, having never sinned, speak from their lofty eminence to those who have. But such is not the tone of those whom Christ has sent; for it is your brethren whom he has appointed, and none else,— sons of Adam, sons of your nature, the same by nature, differing only in grace,—men, like you, exposed to temptations, to the same temptations, to the same warfare within and without; with the same three deadly enemies—the world, the flesh, and the devil; with the same human, the same wayward heart: differing only as the power of God has changed and rules it. So it is; we are not Angels from heaven that speak to you, but men, whom grace, and grace alone, has made to differ from you.

Listen to the Apostle:—When the barbarous Lycaonians, seeing his miracle, would have sacrificed to him and St. Barnabas, as to gods, he rushed in among them, crying out, 'O men, why do ye this? we also are mortals, men like unto you;' or, as the words run more forcibly in the original Greek, 'We are of like passions with you.' And again to the Corinthians he writes, 'We preach not ourselves, but Jesus Christ our Lord; and ourselves your servants through Jesus. God, who commanded the light to shine out of darkness, he hath shined in our hearts, to give the light of the knowledge of the glory of God in the face of Christ Jesus: 'b*ut* we hold this treasure *in earthen vessels.*' And further, he says of himself most wonderfully, that, 'lest he should be exalted by the greatness of the revelations,' there was given him 'an angel of Satan' in his flesh 'to buffet him.' Such are your Ministers, your Preachers, your Priests, O my brethren; not Angels, not Saints, not sinless, but those who would have lived and died in sin except for God's grace, and who, though through God's mercy they be in training for the fellowship of Saints hereafter, yet at present are in the midst of infirmity and temptation, and have no hope, except from the unmerited grace of God, of persevering unto the end.

What a strange, what a striking anomaly is this! All is perfect, all is heavenly, all is glorious, in the dispensation which Christ has vouchsafed us, except the persons of his ministers. He dwells on our altars himself, the Most Holy, the Most High, in light inaccessible, and Angels fall down before him there; and out of visible substances and forms he chooses what is choicest to represent and to hold him. The finest wheat-flour, and the purest wine, are taken as his outward symbols; the most sacred and majestic words minister to the sacrificial rite; altar and sanctuary are adorned decently or splendidly, as our means allow; and the priests perform their office in befitting vestments, lifting up chaste hearts and holy hands; yet those very priests, so set apart, so consecrated, they, with their girdle of celibacy and their maniple of sorrow, are sons of Adam, sons of sinners, of a fallen nature, which they have not put off, though it be renewed through grace, so that it is almost the definition of a priest that he has sins of his own to offer for. 'Every high Priest,' says the Apostle, 'taken from among men, is appointed for men, in the things that appertain unto God, that he may offer gifts and sacrifices for sins; who can condole with those who are in ignorance and error, because he also himself is compassed with infirmity. And therefore he ought, as for the people, so also for himself, to offer for sins.' And hence in the Mass, when he offers up the Host before consecration, he says, *Suscipe, Sancte Pater, Omnipotens, æterne Deus*, 'Accept, Holy Father, Almighty, Everlasting God, this immaculate Host, which I, Thine unworthy servant, offer to Thee, my Living and True God, for *mine* innumerable sins, offences, and negligences, *and* for all who stand around, and for all faithful Christians, living and dead.'

Most strange is this in itself, my brethren, but not strange, when you consider it is the appointment of an all-merciful God; not strange in him, because the Apostle gives the reason of it in the passage I have quoted. The priests of the New Law are men, in order that they may 'condole with those who are in ignorance and error, because they too are compassed with infirmity.' Had Angels been your priests, my brethren, they could not have condoled with you, sympathized with you, have had compassion on you, felt tenderly for you, and made allowances for you, as we can; they could not have been your patterns and guides, and have led you on from your old selves into a new life, as they can who come from the midst of you, who have been led on themselves as you are to be led, who know well your difficulties, who have had experience, at least of your temptations, who know the strength of the flesh and the wiles of the devil, even though they have baffled them, who are already disposed to take your part, and be indulgent towards you, and can advise you most practically, and warn you most seasonably and prudently. Therefore, did he send you men to be the ministers of reconciliation and intercession; as he himself, though he could not sin, yet even he, by becoming man, took on him, as far as was possible to God, man's burden of infirmity and trial in his own person. He could not be a sinner, but he could be a man, and he took to himself a man's heart that we might entrust our hearts to him, and 'was tempted in all things, like as we are, yet without sin.'

Ponder this truth well, my brethren, and let it be your comfort. Among the preachers, among the priests of the Gospel, there have been Apostles, there have been Martyrs, there have been Doctors;—Saints in plenty among them; yet out of them all, high as has been their sanctity, varied their graces, awful their gifts, there has not been one who did not begin with the old Adam; not one of them who was not hewn out of the same rock as the most obdurate of reprobates; not one of them who was not fashioned unto honour out of the same clay which has been the material of the most polluted and vile of sinners; not one who was not by nature brother of those poor souls who have now commenced an eternal fellowship with the devil, and are lost in hell. Grace has vanquished nature; that is the whole history of the Saints. Salutary thought for those who are tempted to pride themselves in what they do, and what they are; wonderful news for those who sorrowfully recognise in their hearts the vast difference that exists between them and the Saints; and joyful news, when men hate sin, and wish to escape from its miserable yoke, yet are tempted to think it impossible!" (Discourse 3. Men, not Angels, the Priests of the Gospel)

Suggested Reading

Apostolic Exhortation Reconciliation and Penance - John Paul II

Screwtape Letters - C.S. Lewis

The Imitation of Christ - Thomas a'Kempis

My Daily Bread

A Treatise on the Particular Examen of Conscience - Luis de la Palma

Frequent Confession - Benedict Baur

Why We Need Confession - Russell Shaw

Peace of Soul – Fulton J. Sheen

The Return of the Prodigal Son – Henri J.M. Nouwen

Wounds that Heal – Deacon Keith A. Fournier

I Will Give Them a New Heart – Conrad W. Baars, M.D.

Healing the Unaffirmed – Conrad W. Baars, M.D. and Ann A. Terruwe, M.D.

Intimacy and the Hungers of the Heart – Pat Collins, C.M.

CHAPTER FIVE

THIS IS MY BODY. THIS IS MY BLOOD.

Through John Meehan's leadership, Magdalen College always made the Catholic Mass and Eucharistic devotion the center of the college. A meticulous following of the Vatican II liturgical reform has been the jewel of the foundation and history of Magdalen College. When we were in our second year at Magdalen College, many of us made the life changing decision to attend Mass every day.

We need to be totally convinced that Jesus remains with us in the tabernacle of every Catholic Church. His Real Presence is celebrated and adored in the monstrance placed in every chapel dedicated to perpetual adoration. He is with us, not just spiritually, but physically as well. This is the miracle of the Eucharist.

When a Catholic priest takes a little piece of unleavened bread and repeats the words that Jesus spoke at the Last Supper, *"This is my body,"* and when he takes a small of amount of wine in a chalice and says, *"This is my blood,"* the bread is no longer bread and the wine is no longer wine.

At every Holy Sacrifice of the Mass, we participate in a marvelous miracle, the miracle called Transubstantiation. The Catechism of the Catholic Church explains this miracle when it says:

"The mode of Christ's presence under the Eucharistic species is unique. It raises the Eucharist above all the sacraments as the perfection of the spiritual life and the end to which all the sacraments tend. In the most blessed sacrament of the Eucharist the body and blood, together with the soul and divinity of our Lord Jesus Christ and, therefore, the whole Christ is truly, really and substantially contained. This presence is called real – by which is not intended to exclude the other types of presence as if they could not be real too, but because it is presence in the fullest sense: that is to say, it is a substantial presence by which Christ, God and man, makes himself wholly and entirely present" (#1374).

Transubstantiation cannot be proved through scientific experimentation. If we were to examine reverently a consecrated host using a high-powered microscope lens, the physical attributes of bread would be obvious. If we were to do to the same with the precious blood, the physical attributes would be that of wine.

Transubstantiation belongs to the reality of faith. Faith does not contradict reason. Instead, the gift of faith that we receive at Baptism, gives us a superior vision.

Transubstantiation means "change of substance" or "change of reality." When the priest repeats the words that Jesus spoke at the Last Supper, the bread is no longer bread, and the wine is no longer wine. Instead, the entire substance of the bread and the entire substance of the wine have been changed into the substance of The Body and Blood of Christ. Transubstantiation occurs only by the power of God, and in a way that we cannot empirically detect. We know that Transubstantiation takes place through the certainty of faith. Jesus, the Son of God; Jesus the Messiah; Jesus the Lord and Savior of the universe said: *"This is my body;" "This is my blood."* Faith is a vision superior to reason, but it does not contradict reason, precisely because faith relies upon the authority of God who does not deceive, nor can be deceived. Jesus is the Truth and thus is incapable of lying.

Although Transubstantiation belongs to the reality of faith, from time to time God provides empirical scientific proof of this mystery of our faith. One such reminder took place in 1263. A German priest, Peter of Prague, stopped at Bolsena while on a pilgrimage to Rome. He is described as being a pious priest, but one who found it difficult to believe in Transubstantiation. While celebrating Mass at the tomb of St. Christina, located in Bolsena, Italy, he had barely spoken the words of Consecration when blood started to seep from the consecrated Host and trickle over his hands onto the altar and the corporal.

The priest was immediately confused. At first he attempted to hide the blood, but then he interrupted the Mass and asked to be taken to the neighboring city of Orvieto, the city where Pope Urban IV was then residing.

The Pope listened to the priest's story and gave him absolution for his lack of faith. He then sent emissaries for an immediate investigation. When all the facts were ascertained, he ordered the Bishop of the diocese to bring to Orvieto the Host and the linen cloth bearing the stains of blood. With archbishops, cardinals and other Church dignitaries in attendance, the Pope met the procession and, amid great pomp, had the relics placed in the cathedral. The linen corporal bearing the spots of blood is still reverently enshrined and exhibited in the Cathedral of Orvieto, Italy.

Pope Urban IV was prompted by this miracle to commission Saint Thomas Aquinas to compose the liturgical prayers in honor of the

Eucharist. One year after the miracle, in August of 1264, Pope Urban IV introduced the saint's compositions, and by means of a papal bull instituted the feast of Corpus Christi.

We also must take into account the writings of the Church Fathers.

As early as 110 A.D., St. Ignatius of Antioch said: "Take note of those who hold heterodox opinions on the grace of Jesus Christ which has come to us, and see how contrary their opinions are to the mind of God. They abstain from the Eucharist and from prayer because they do not confess that the Eucharist is the flesh of our Savior Jesus Christ, flesh that suffered for our sins and which that Father, in his goodness, raised up again. They who deny the gift of God are perishing in their disputes" (Letter to the Smyrnaeans 6:2–7:1).

Around the year 151 A.D., St. Justin wrote to the Roman Emperor Antoninus Pius these words: "We call this food Eucharist, and no one else is permitted to partake of it, except one who believes our teaching to be true and who has been washed in the washing which is for the remission of sins and for regeneration [i.e., has received Baptism] and is thereby living as Christ enjoined. For not as common bread nor common drink do we receive these; but since Jesus Christ our Savior was made incarnate by the word of God and had both flesh and blood for our salvation, so too, as we have been taught, the food which has been made into the Eucharist by the Eucharistic prayer set down by him, and by the change of which our blood and flesh is nurtured, is both the flesh and the blood of that incarnated Jesus" (First Apology 66).

Every time we gaze upon him, every time Our Lord and Savior enters our bodies and souls through Holy Communion, he tells us to be wise, and not to be foolish and ignorant. He tells us to follow him, to put into practice his way of life so that we may gain eternal life in Heaven.

"Amen, amen, I say to you, unless you eat the flesh of the Son of Man and drink His blood, you do not have life within you. Whoever eats my flesh and drinks my blood has eternal life, and I will raise him on the last day. For my flesh is true food, and my blood is true drink" (John 6: 52-55).

As John Paul II so eloquently taught us in his first encyclical letter, Jesus reveals man to himself. Jesus is the perfect man who shows us exactly how we must live out our daily lives. Jesus embodies every human and spiritual virtue. The true disciple of Jesus must take him as the model and make his teaching the criterion for every human thought and action undertaken.

"The man who wishes to understand himself thoroughly - and not just in accordance with immediate, partial, often superficial, and even illusory standards and measures of his being – he must with his unrest, uncertainty and even his weakness and sinfulness, with his life and death, draw near to Christ. He must, so to speak, enter into him with all his own self, he must 'appropriate' and assimilate the whole reality of the Incarnation and Redemption in order to find himself." (Pope John Paul II, *Redemptor Hominis*)

Each time we come to the Eucharist, it is Jesus himself who not only shows us how to live our lives, but who also provides us with the divine grace to live out the gospel teachings in our daily existence.

This is why we must have a daily Eucharistic life. Each time we have contact with our Eucharistic Lord, we become one with him. We assimilate him into our being. Holy Communion becomes a communion of two persons and thus, transformation takes place. Only the foolish and the ignorant would stay away from the greatest gift that Jesus has given to us.

I urge you to center your life on the Eucharist. Go to Mass every day. If that is objectively impossible, then make a daily visit to the Blessed Sacrament.

Dr. Scott Hahn, the famous former Protestant minister that converted to Catholicism wrote in his conversion story one of the most beautiful testimonies about the Eucharist that I have ever read. Here are his words, written in his book that he co-authored with his wife Kimberly:

"Then one day, I made a 'fatal blunder' – I decided that it was time for me to go to Mass on my own. Finally I resolved to darken the doors of Gesu, Marquette University's parish. Right before noon, I slipped quietly into the basement chapel for daily Mass. I wasn't sure what to expect; maybe I'd be alone with a priest and a couple of old nuns. I took a seat as an observer in the back pew.

All of a sudden lots of ordinary people began coming in off the streets; rank-and-file type folks. They came in, genuflected, knelt and prayed. Their simple but sincere devotion was impressive.

Then a bell rang and a priest walked out toward the altar. I remained seated; I still wasn't sure if it was safe to kneel. As an evangelical

Calvinist, I had been taught that the Catholic Mass was the greatest sacrilege that a man could commit - to re-sacrifice Christ - so I wasn't sure what to do.

I watched and listened as the readings, prayers and responses - so steeped in Scripture - made the Bible come alive. I almost wanted to stop the Mass and say, 'Wait. That line is from Isaiah; the song is from the Psalms. Whoa, you've got another prophet in that prayer'. I found numerous elements from the ancient Jewish liturgy that I had studied so intensely.

All of a sudden I realized, this is where the Bible belongs. This was the setting in which this precious family heirloom was meant to be read, proclaimed and expounded. Then we moved into the Liturgy of the Eucharist, where all my covenant conclusions converged.

I wanted to stop everything and shout, 'Hey, can I explain what's happening from Scripture? This is great!' Instead I just sat there, famished with a supernatural hunger for the Bread of Life.

After pronouncing the words of consecration, the priest held up the Host. I felt as if the last drop of doubt had drained from me. With all of my heart, I whispered, 'My Lord and my God. That's really you! And if that's you, then I want full communion with you. I don't want to hold anything back" (Rome Sweet Home, pp. 87-88).

Our belief in the Real Presence must permeate all of our actions when we are in church. Silence, reverent genuflections, proper attire and punctuality for worship are all manifestations of deep respect and faith. All of these things were insisted upon at Magdalen College. Liturgical life at college was something very serious, but very joyful as well.

The Eucharist is called Holy Communion. Jesus himself, through the Eucharist, grants to us the most powerful experience of intimacy possible within our earthly existence. As Pope Benedict explains: "And that is what is really happening in Communion, that we allow ourselves to be drawn into him, into his inner communion, and are thus led finally into a state of inner resemblance" (God and the World.

Many Catholics throughout the world no longer believe in the Real Presence. What could be a cause of this alarming loss of faith in something so basic to Catholicism?

Cardinal Joseph Ratzinger, now our beloved Pope Benedict XVI, provides an interesting answer to this question. He writes, "Johann Baptist Metz once said that the formula today is: No to God, yes to religion. People want to have some kind of religion, esoteric or whatever it may be. But a personal God, who speaks to me, who knows me personally, who has said something quite specific and who has met me with a specific demand, and who will also judge me – people don't want him. What we see is religion being separated from God. People don't want to do without this sensation of the Wholly Other, this special religious feeling, entirely; they want it available in many shapes and forms. But there is in the end no guarantee of its continuing to be there, unless the will of God and God himself are also present. In that sense we are not so much in the middle of a religious crisis – religions are springing up all over the place – as in the middle of a God crisis" (God and the World, p. 69)

Look at the tabernacle. Our Lord is truly there. He looks at you and cries out: *"All you who are thirsty, come to the water! You who have no money, come, receive grain and eat; Come, without paying and without cost, drink wine and milk! Why spend your money for what is not bread; your wages for what fails to satisfy?"* (Isaiah 55: 1-2)

What intimacy! When Jesus comes to us, he comes to us as communion. God and man become one. He comes to us as the Divine Lover. His communion with us is more intimate than the intimate union of husband and wife or a mother with her unborn child.

We cannot even begin to fathom the depth of God's love for us. His love is so immense that he himself is defined as love. *"God is love"* (1 John 4: 8, 16). The Eucharist is the most visible sign of God's love for each of us. Jesus loves us so much that he cannot leave us. *"And know that I am with you always until the end of time"* (Matthew 28: 20).

As we consider the mystery of God's unconditional love we are reminded that love defines the very purpose of our existence too. The purpose of our life can be summed up with only one word: love. *"...since God has loved us so much, we too should love one another"* (1 John 4: 11).

The human person cannot live without the experience of divine love and human love. The human person cannot live without the experience of divine intimacy and human intimacy. The human person cannot live without communion. Man becomes fully realized in communion because he is created for communion by a God who is the most perfect communion.

"Man cannot live without love. He remains a being that is incomprehensible for himself, his life is senseless, if love is not revealed to him, if he does not encounter love, if he does not experience it and make it his own, if he does not participate intimately in it" (John Paul II, The Redeemer of Man, 10.1).

When it comes to the Eucharist, the bottom line is this: either Jesus Christ is the Incarnate Word of God, or he is a complete and total lunatic. Either the Catholic Church possesses the greatest gift known to humanity, or we are idol worshippers.

Personally, I have never doubted. However, I think that aside from the volumes of beautiful theology and spirituality that have been written about the Eucharist, and even aside from the countless number of our brothers and sisters, who throughout the centuries, have shed their blood to defend the Eucharist, my favorite proof of the Eucharist is contained in the sixth chapter of the Gospel of Saint John.

Had Jesus been telling his disciples that the Eucharist was merely a symbol of his presence among us, he would have begun calling after them, asking that they return even as they were departing from his company. He would have attempted to explain his words to them and to assure them that they must have misunderstood him. Instead, what did he do? He stood firm and watched them leave.

Then with majesty and self-dominion he turned to his Apostles and asked an amazing question: *"Will you also go away?"* (John 6: 67). Without hesitation, Peter, the first Pope of the Catholic Church, pronounced some of the most powerful words of the Bible: *"Master, to whom shall we go? You have the words of eternal life. We have come to believe and are convinced that you are the Holy One of God"* (John 6: 68-69).

The real difficulty in accepting Catholicism is two-fold. Catholicism demands an act of total surrender to Jesus with a complete acceptance of him as the final authority; and Catholicism also demands a moral standard of the highest level. The difficulty for the first disciples and for many of his disciples today, is to accept the Eucharist as true, with all its implications. Many refuse Christ, not because he puzzles the intellect, but because he challenges our lives.

Every Sunday or even during the week, we worship at our parishes and receive the gift of the Eucharist without even considering the thousands upon thousands of our brothers and sisters who throughout the history of the Catholic Church have given their lives precisely to defend what we do without any obstacles at all. Here is one story that is very moving and happened not too far from our own country.

An excellent book by Joan Carrol Cruz called *Saintly Women of Modern Times* narrates a story that took place during the 1920's when there was a brutal persecution against the Catholic Church throughout Mexico. Churches were closed and the land was drenched with the blood of thousands of martyrs made up of priests, religious and lay people. The persecution went on for the next two decades and even to this day, there are many vestiges of a pervasive anti-catholic mentality.

One group of ladies, among many examples of heroism that were prevalent throughout Mexico, showed their love for their parish priest one day in 1934.

Maria de la Luz Camacho, an attractive twenty-seven year old woman was standing by the front doors of her parish church of Coyoacan, Mexico. Maria led a group of young women to guard the church because she had learned that a large group of men from the anti-Catholic Red Syndicate had planned to burn down the church, carry the priest off to jail or even kill him.

When the group of revolutionaries arrived at the parish church, Maria, her sister, and a small group of valiant young women stood at the doors of the church. "We are not afraid. If it becomes necessary, we are ready to die for Christ the King," cried out Maria. "Those who wish to enter this church must first pass over my body." Shortly after the initial confrontation, the Red Shirts opened fire and Maria de la Luz Camacho was killed.

Word spread quickly about her martyrdom. 30,000 people assembled in the small town for her funeral. Even the archbishop of Mexico City, Pascual Diaz Barreto, joined the procession and led the funeral rites. He was overcome with emotion as he witnessed such a large crowd assemble without fear of the government.

As a priest, I would be willing to shed my blood for my parishioners. Would you be willing to shed your blood to protect the Eucharist and your priest?

Today the Catholic Church is under attack. A "Trojan horse" filled with many members of the clergy who prefer to imitate Judas rather than the Master has infiltrated the ranks of the Catholic priesthood. In the "Trojan horse" are also many lay Catholics who are "avid for the latest novelty and collect for themselves a whole series of teachers according to their own tastes" (see 2 Timothy 4: 1-5).

The same courage that Maria de la Luz Camacho displayed is the same kind of courage that is needed today. We need to imitate great Catholic saints and martyrs like Athanasius, John Fisher, Thomas More and Edmund Campion who all stood firm and alone during difficult times in the history of the Catholic Church.

I have never really understood why people who could attend Mass or make Eucharistic visits during the week simply choose not to do so. It is quite possible that with the availability of so many parishes and adoration chapels, that people simply begin to take the gift of the Eucharist for granted or they simply do not have enough faith.

However, what would happen if you were in a prolonged situation where you did not have the regular availability of a priest? What would happen if even Sunday Mass was no longer accessible?

Many of our brothers and sisters throughout the world experience these kinds of terrible situations. One example can be found in the life of Francis Xavier Nguyen Van Thuan.

Francis was a Catholic priest from Vietnam. He became a bishop in 1975 and later was chosen to be a cardinal. Only a few months after he became a bishop, he was arrested by the Vietnamese government and imprisoned for thirteen years. Nine of those thirteen years were spent in solitary confinement!

During the Jubilee Year 2000, Pope John Paul II invited the Cardinal Van Thuan to direct the annual Lenten spiritual exercises for himself and the Curia. The collection of meditations that were delivered make up an amazing book entitled *Testimony of Hope.*

In one of the meditations, Cardinal Francis Xavier Nguyen Van Thuan movingly describes what it was like not to have the Eucharist readily available and what he had to do to celebrate Mass.

"When I was arrested, I had to leave immediately with empty hands. The next day, I was permitted to write to my people in order to ask for the most necessary things: clothes, toothpaste…I wrote, 'Please send me a little wine as medicine for my stomach ache.' The faithful understood right away.

They sent me a small bottle of wine for Mass with a label that read, 'medicine for stomachaches.' They also sent some hosts, which they hid in a flashlight for protection against the humidity. The police asked me, 'You have stomach aches? Yes. Here's some medicine for you.'

I never will be able to express my great joy! Every day, with three drops of wine and a drop of water in the palm of my hand, I would celebrate Mass. This was my altar, and this was my cathedral! It was true medicine for soul and body, 'Medicine of immortality, remedy so as not to die but to have life always in Jesus', as St. Ignatius of Antioch says.

Each time I celebrated the Mass, I had the opportunity to extend my hands and nail myself to the cross with Jesus, to drink with him the bitter chalice. Each day in reciting the words of consecration, I confirmed with all my heart and soul a new pact, and eternal pact between Jesus and me through his blood mixed with mine. Those were the most beautiful Masses of my life!" (p. 131)

One final thought about the Eucharist: never receive the Eucharist in the state of mortal sin. Please take very seriously the words of Saint Paul: *"Everyone is to recollect himself before eating this bread and drinking this cup; because a person who eats and drinks without recognizing the Body is eating and drinking his own condemnation. In fact, that is why many of you are weak and ill and some of you have died. If we only recollected ourselves, we should not be punished like that. But when the Lord does punish us like that, it is to correct us and stop us from being condemned with the world"* (1 Corinthians 11: 28-32).

Suggested Reading

The Mystery of Faith – Pope Paul VI

Dominicae Cenae – John Paul II

The Lamb's Supper – Scott Hahn

Eucharistic Miracles – Joan Carroll Cruz

The Cure of Ars and the Holy Eucharist – St. John Vianney

Life of Christ – Fulton J. Sheen

The Lord – Romano Guardini

The Spirit of the Liturgy – Joseph Ratzinger

CHAPTER SIX

HOW TO KEEP YOUR SANITY IN AN INSANE WORLD

"It was the best of times, it was the worst of times, it was the age of wisdom, it was the age of foolishness, it was the epoch of belief, it was the epoch of incredulity, it was the season of Light, it was the season of Darkness, it was the spring of hope, it was the winter of despair, we had everything before us, we had nothing before us, we were all going direct to heaven, we were all going direct the other way - in short, the period was so far like the present period, that some of its noisiest authorities insisted on its being received, for good or for evil, in the superlative degree of comparison only."

Charles Dickens words at the beginning of *A Tale of Two Cities* can describe most periods of human history. His words certainly apply to the times that we live in.

Only the blind and the apathetic would assert that our times are not challenging. We do live in a time of upheaval.

It is easy for many to become discouraged. However, this is not a possible response for those who call themselves true disciples of Jesus Christ.

"Then I saw a new heaven and a new earth; the first heaven and the first earth had disappeared now, and there was no longer any sea. I saw the holy city, and the new Jerusalem, coming down from God out of heaven, as beautiful as a bride all dressed for her husband. Then I heard a loud voice call from the throne, 'You see this city? Here God lives among men. He will make his home among them; they shall be his people, and he will be their God; his name is God-with-them. He will wipe away all tears from their eyes, there will be no more death, and no more mourning or sadness. The world of the past has gone'" (Revelation 21: 1-4).

Serious Catholics are overwhelmed by the meltdowns around us. Many are alarmed by the ever increasing collapse of the Catholic Church in this country. In some parts of the country parishes are closing at an alarming rate. Clergy scandals continue and the dwindling ranks of priests are replaced by foreign priests that nobody can understand.

A Muslim extremist wipes out a room full of American soldiers while our bravest men and women continue to fight a war that has no exit strategy or clear plan for victory. National politics has become alarmingly polarized as radicals attempt to change our great nation into a European-style socialist state.

Meanwhile, the country continues to morally spin out of control because we have forgotten God. British historian and philosopher Arnold Toynbee (1889-1975) once said: "Civilizations die from suicide, not by murder."

Nevertheless, within all of these challenges, there are many signs of hope and renewal.

I once discussed my concerns with one of my parishioners, a Filipino nurse. Speaking with her characteristic brevity and clarity she said, "Father, those who are in are in, and those who are out are out."

More and more people, especially young people and young families are living the Catholic Faith with maturity, authenticity and joy. They are open to life, attending Mass every day, praying the Rosary and standing in line for confession. They are the pillars of parish life and they are committed to the pro-life movement. These are the people who not only remain active in the political process; they are bringing the message to the steps of the politicians.

Married couples open to life are creating the culture of life envisioned by Pope John Paul II.

Recently I asked Matthew Matl, a parishioner and the oldest of six children, what he thought of his mother bringing a new addition into their family. Matthew's face lit up and said, "This is so awesome. Now we are tied with the Metz's". John and Virginia Metz have seven children. Other families too, in my parish, provide an awesome testimony of their love for life.

Religious orders that are faithful to the Magisterium and Bishops who are faithful to the Church are attracting large numbers of young and enthusiastic vocations.

Institutions and organizations come and go. Too many people have too many expectations in leaders and renewal movements within the Church. They see these apostolic works as an answer to the meltdown, but they are let down by their flawed leaders.

Our hope is in Jesus Christ the Lord, not in organizations and human leaders.

The collapse and failed attempts of renewal by different institutions could be a wakeup call from God. Is it possible that within the storm peace can be found through detachment?

What is detachment? Without getting too complicated and too theological, detachment basically means that we love God more than we love people, places and things. God has to be first. Do you love money, your car, your house, your clothes or your job more than God? Detachment, though, does not mean that we become unconcerned about our family, work and the needs of others.

I believe that the Catholic Church, through the Second Vatican Council, has called us to live a new spirituality. Rather than fleeing from the concerns of the world, we are to immerse ourselves into the world and attempt to make it a better place for everyone. We are to feed the hungry, give drink to the thirsty, clothe the naked, shelter the homeless, visit the sick, visit those in prison, bury the dead, convert the sinner, instruct the ignorant, counsel the doubtful, comfort the sorrowful, bear wrongs patiently, forgive injuries and pray for the living and the dead. However, all of this must be done with a profound sense of detachment.

"Therefore, while we are warned that it profits a man nothing if he gain the whole world and lose himself, the expectation of a new earth must not weaken but rather stimulate our concern for cultivating this one. For here grows the body of a new human family, a body which even now is able to give some kind of foreshadowing of the new age" (Second Vatican Council, *Gaudium et spes*, 39).

Detachment means that we are to love God above all other persons, places and things. *"Seek first the kingdom of God and all these things will be given to you"* (Matthew 6: 33). Jesus does not tell us to only love God, he tells us to love God first. All other loves must be subordinated to our first love. To love God first requires a profound spiritual life and a lot of mortification.

The beautiful prayer of Saint Ignatius Loyola called the *Suscipe* can help us live out the virtue of detachment. "Receive, O Lord, all my liberty. Take my memory, my understanding and my entire will. Whatsoever I have or hold, you have given me; I give it back to you and surrender it wholly to be governed by your will. Give me only your love and your grace, with these I will be rich enough and ask for nothing more."

Detachment does not mean that we are supposed to retreat from the world and live on islands. Detachment does mean that we are to love intensely without clinging to people, places or things. Material things such as a house, a car, money, our education and a computer are means to bring about greater human progress. We can enjoy the use of these things immensely so long as they do not distract us from our first love. Our career should be seen through the prism of detachment. Work becomes a means of personal sanctification and it allows us to use our work to help others. Employers create jobs and profits can be used to help others.

I am always moved by these words from the *Eucharistic Prayer for Masses for Various Needs and Occasions III*: "Keep your Church alert in faith to the signs of the times and eager to accept the challenge of the gospel. Open our hearts to the needs of all humanity, so that sharing their grief and anguish, their joy and hope, we may faithfully bring them the good news of salvation and advance together on the way to your kingdom."

Today, most people deal with dysfunctional family situations. Parents suffer tremendously because some or all of their children just do not get it. Many children suffer a lot too, because their parents are dysfunctional.

We can find peace even within these very difficult family situations through detachment. Continue to love everyone, but do not cling to them. Love them with all of their wounds. Accept the burdens of their limitations. This is what Jesus does for them. Through a deep spiritual life, compassion and patience will accompany a spirit of detachment. Imitate the example of the Good Samaritan.

I have always admired Saint Francis of Assisi. As I grow older, his example inspires me all the more.

When his father denounced him publicly in front of the Bishop and the bystanders that gathered in the plaza, Francis removed his clothes and stood naked in front of everyone. This rather extreme act, so characteristic of Francis' method of getting a point across (he was quite a dramatic Italian), symbolized his total detachment from everyone and everything.

Francis did not leave the world; rather he immersed himself into all of creation. His passion was to change his world by preaching the Gospel. He preached the Gospel by living it.

Before Jesus called him "to rebuild my Church", Francis had a deep friendship with Clare. He continued to love Clare, but in a pure and detached manner. Clare was to follow Francis' example by becoming a nun and later founded her own religious order. Although separated by her calling, they remained friends for life. Their love for each other was always subordinated to their first love. As Antoine de Saint-Exupéry wrote that "being in love does not mean looking at each other, but looking together in the same direction."

Francis' public nakedness symbolized the manner he walked through his world. Although physically clothed, he was spiritually naked loving all creatures without clinging to any of them. This way of journeying through the world, required of Francis a profound love for God and immense mortification.

In his Canticle, St. Francis prays:

Most High, all-powerful, all-good Lord,
All praise is Yours, all glory, all honor and all blessings.
To you alone, Most High, do they belong,
and no mortal lips are worthy to pronounce Your Name.

Praised be You my Lord with all Your creatures,
especially Sir Brother Sun,
Who is the day through whom You give us light.
And he is beautiful and radiant with great splendor,
Of You Most High, he bears the likeness.

Praised be You, my Lord, through Sister Moon and the stars,

In the heavens you have made them bright, precious and fair.

Praised be You, my Lord, through Brothers Wind and Air,
And fair and stormy, all weather's moods,
by which You cherish all that You have made.

Praised be You my Lord through Sister Water,
So useful, humble, precious and pure.

Praised be You my Lord through Brother Fire,
through whom You light the night
and he is beautiful and playful and robust and strong.

Praised be You my Lord through our Sister,
Mother Earth
who sustains and governs us,
producing varied fruits with colored flowers and herbs.
Praise be You my Lord through those who grant pardon
for love of You and bear sickness and trial.
Blessed are those who endure in peace,
By You Most High, they will be crowned.

Praised be You, my Lord through Sister Death,
from whom no-one living can escape.

Woe to those who die in mortal sin!
Blessed are they She finds doing Your Will.
No second death can do them harm.
Praise and bless my Lord and give Him thanks,
And serve Him with great humility.

It might be comfortable to retreat from this turbulent and chaotic world. But, even the monks and cloistered nuns are evangelizing the world from their monasteries by their prayers and sacrifices.

Experience has shown me that forgiveness is the deepest expression of detachment. To forgive someone for an injury that we have received is a profound act of letting go. Nevertheless, we can never forget what happened. We cannot erase our memory. Forgiving and forgetting are not the same.

The fact that we cannot forget is good because the memory of the past allows us to establish boundaries in our relationships with others. Our memory allows us to be more prudent and to accept the limitations of others with compassion.

I am shocked when I watch old movies that depict the life of the Catholic Church. Movies that show children running around all over the sacristy and the rectory are from the days of innocence when no one could fathom the scandals of today.

However, perhaps a lot of the clergy abuse scandals could have been avoided if greater boundaries were established. Bad apples were around even years ago. Caution may have prevented bad priests from taking advantage of certain situations.

I was a member of the Legionaries of Christ for twenty-one years. My formation and experience were extremely positive. No one ever suspected that the founder of our religious order lived a terribly scandalous and double life. We never saw anything that would cause suspicion.

I have forgiven Father Maciel, but I will never get involved with a large group of priests again until true and lasting reforms take place within the Catholic Church. Forgiveness is one thing, forgetfulness is another.

Abraham Lincoln said it best when he said, "You can fool some of the people all of the time, and all of the people some of the time, but you cannot fool all of the people all of the time."

Meltdowns do not anger me anymore. The disasters allow me to get closer to God and to keep doing my ministry as a priest with greater joy and greater interior freedom.

Consider for a moment the first words of Jesus from the Cross: "Father, forgive them, for they do not know what they are doing" (Luke 23: 34). Even from the Cross, Jesus continued to love without any restrictions.

Pain and suffering may tempt us to give up on humanity, but as I have already said, the Catholic Church is calling us not to give up. Pope John Paul II challenged us to be part of the new evangelization; a new springtime for the Church. However, spring means that snow, ice and mud are still on the ground. Flowers and leaves are just beginning to bud.

The Catholic Church in America will become smaller and more faithful. Our nation will become something different. All of the traditional structures of support that have made our lives comfortable and easy are presently engulfed in confusion, but transformation is slowly taking place. Without daily contemplative prayer and daily Mass, or at least a prolonged visit before the Blessed Sacrament, you will be overpowered by anxiety and fear. You will implode without a personal relationship with God.

"From the crisis of today the Church of tomorrow will emerge a Church that has lost much. She will become small and will have to start afresh more or less from the beginning. She will no longer be able to inhabit many of the edifices that she built in prosperity. As the number of her adherents diminishes, so will she lose many of her social privileges. In contrast to an earlier age, she will be seen much more as a voluntary society, entered only by free decision. As a small society, she will make much bigger demands on the initiative of her individual members. Undoubtedly she will discover new forms of ministry and will ordain to the priesthood approved Christians who pursue some profession. In many smaller congregations or in self-contained social groups, pastoral care will be normally provided in this fashion. Alongside this, the full-time ministry of the priesthood will be indispensable as formerly. But in all of the changes at which one might guess, the Church will find her essence afresh and with full conviction in that which was always at her center: faith in the triune God, in Jesus Christ, the Son of God made man, the presence of the Spirit until the end of the world. In faith and prayer she will again recognize her true center and experience the sacraments again as the worship of God and not as a subject for liturgical scholarship" (Pope Benedict XVI, Faith and the Future, pp. 116-117).

A contemporary spiritual writer describes the qualities of this new relationship with God when he writes, "This adventure of faith will consist in burning bridges, setting aside all rules of common sense and all probabilities and, like Abraham, disregarding arguments, explanations and proofs, untying ourselves from all rational positions and, bound hand and foot, making the great leap into the abyss of the dark night, surrendering ourselves to the totally Other-God Alone-in pure and dark faith.

The contemplative of the future will need to enter the unfathomable regions of the mystery of God-without guides, without supports, without light. God will be experienced as the Other Limit; God's distance and proximity will be meditated upon simultaneously; and as a result, there will be a feeling of dizziness which is a mixture of fascination, fright, annihilation and dread.

The contemplative will have to run the risk of being submerged in this bottomless ocean where dangerous challenges are hidden. These, the contemplative cannot shun, but must face and accept them in their burning insistency.

Those who return from this adventure will be figures sculpted by purity, strength, and fire. Transformed by the ecstatic closeness of God, above them will appear the living and illuminating image of the Son. They will become the transparent witnesses of God" (Ignacio Larrañaga, Sensing

Your Hidden Presence: Toward Intimacy with God, p. 12).

Moments of silence and solitude are necessary. The craziness around us will drain our energies. Getting away from everything for a day, a weekend or a week or two is necessary.

Ray is very generous with his time. Every year he successfully organizes a city-wide fund raising event for the pro-life organizations of the area and he is the chairman of the board of Hope House, a home for unwed mothers with crisis pregnancies. His mission does not consist simply of a monthly Hope House meeting. He is intimately involved in the day to day operations of the home and he spends a lot of time writing grant requests for the shelter.

Aside from his involvement with the pro-life movement, Ray is one of the pillars of my parish and he serves as the chairman of our Finance Council. He holds a full time job at the local military base and he is very devoted to his family. He always has a joyful and positive demeanor.

What is his secret? Frequently he takes his boat to Baffin Bay, a scenic portion of the Gulf of Mexico and he goes fishing usually alone. The solitude, the silence and the joy of the sport recharges his batteries so that he can continue giving of himself to others with a profound sense of dedication and charity.

Sometimes people question why I leave my parish periodically in order to write my books. Like Ray's fishing trips, writing has become a source of renewal. In order to maintain my characteristic enthusiasm and a high-energy level in my mission as a pastor of a new and growing parish, prolonged moments of solitude and silence are essential. The ocean provides the backdrop where the Holy Spirit renews me. I would like to tell you about the beautiful places that I have found in Mexico, but then I would have to kill you.

"The prophets of God are forged on the anvil of solitude: there, on the burning coals, they endure the gaze of God without blinking, and when they descend to the plains, they transmit splendor, spirit and life. In the silence of the desert, they 'saw and heard' something, and once again among the people, no one can silence their voices. They perceived something, and there is no one in the world who can destroy their testimony, and invariably, they are transformed into trumpets of the Invisible that cannot be silenced. The masses know how to distinguish between one who is sent and a meddler" (Ignacio Larrañaga, Sensing Your Hidden Presence: Toward Intimacy with God, p. 113).

The challenges of today demand of us also to trust in God completely. Let us recall the words that Jesus spoke during the Sermon on the Mount.

"That is why I am telling you not to worry about your life and what you are to eat, nor about your body and what you are to wear. Surely life is more than food, and the body more than clothing! Look at the birds in the sky. They do not sow or reap or gather into barns; yet your heavenly Father feeds them. Are you not worth much more than they are? Can any of you, however much you worry, add one single cubit to your span of life? And why worry about clothing? Think of the flowers growing in the fields; they never have to work or spin; yet I assure you that not even Solomon in all his royal robes was clothed like one of these. Now if that is how God clothes the wild flowers growing in the field which are there today and thrown into the furnace tomorrow, will he not much more look after you, you who have so little faith? So do not worry; do not say, 'What are we to eat? What are we to drink? What are we to wear?' It is the gentiles who set their hearts on all these things. Your heavenly Father knows you need them all. Set

your hearts on his kingdom first, and on God's saving justice and all these other things will be given you as well. So do not worry about tomorrow: tomorrow will take care of itself. Each day has enough trouble of its own" (Matthew 6: 25-34).

Detachment, forgiveness, silence and trust in God – these are the components of a contemporary spirituality for today. If you embark upon this journey, you will be filled with joy and hope – gaudium et spes.

Going back to St. Francis of Assisi, let us finish this chapter with a beautiful prayer which is attributed to the founder of the Franciscans. Not only should this prayer be a part of your daily spiritual life, it needs to be a program that it is lived within the daily circumstances of our difficult world.

Lord, make me an instrument of your peace,
Where there is hatred, let me sow love;
where there is injury, pardon;
where there is doubt, faith;
where there is despair, hope;
where there is darkness, light;
where there is sadness, joy;

O Divine Master, grant that I may not so much seek
to be consoled as to console;
to be understood as to understand;
to be loved as to love.

For it is in giving that we receive;
it is in pardoning that we are pardoned;
and it is in dying that we are born to eternal life.

Suggested Reading

Crossing the Threshold of Hope – John Paul II

Saint Francis of Assisi – G.K. Chesterton

Testimony of Hope – Francis Xavier Nguyen Van Thuan

The Courage to Be Catholic – George Weigel

The End of the Present World and the Mysteries of the Future Life – Charles Arminjon

Awareness – Anthony De Mello

Walking on Water – Anthony De Mello

Compassion – Henry Nouwen, Donald P. McNeill and Douglas A. Morrison

CHAPTER SEVEN

ENJOYING LIFE

It seems to me that God knew what he was doing when he made the Sabbath. *"On the seventh day God had completed the work he had been doing. He rested on the seventh day after the work he had been doing. God blessed the seventh day and made it holy, because on that day he rested after all his work of creating"* (Genesis 2: 1-3).

As soon as Sunday became a day like any other day of the week, America went down the tubes. Without the Sabbath most people lost their relationship with their Creator. Without the Sabbath most people lost their relationship with their family. Without the Sabbath neighborhoods filled with kids riding their bicycles, playing baseball, or building tree forts have become things of the past.

The Sabbath reminds us of our relationship with God and it keeps us together as a family, a Church, and as a country. The Sabbath rest fosters personal holiness. The reminder comes from the fact that Sunday is different. It is the Sabbath. We go to Mass. We do not work. We spend time with family and friends. The weekly Sabbath rest allows us to be fully human. It is through the Sabbath rest that we renew ourselves in God, family and friends.

In my home we never missed Mass on Sunday. Preparation for Sunday morning Mass began on Saturday night. My Dad worked long and hard hours at his restaurant every day of the week except for Sundays. As a child I can remember how he would ask me just about every Saturday evening to polish his dress shoes for Sunday Mass. We all had clothes that were only used for Sunday Mass. My Mom instructed us each Saturday night how to lay out our clothes for the following morning.

After Sunday morning Mass, my Mom always prepared a huge Sunday dinner. Both my Mom and Dad are fabulous in the kitchen. It was very common that my maternal grandparents and great-grandparents would join us just about every Sunday. My paternal grandparents would join us whenever they could. They used to bring over the most delicious Italian pastries. These are six people that I miss a lot. They have all gone to the eternal Sabbath, but the memories are profound precisely because we always celebrated the Sabbath in time and space.

My Mom was always the social leader of our family and our neighborhood. On Christmas,

Easter and Thanksgiving our house was always packed with relatives and friends.

My hometown of Ridgefield, Connecticut is still known to this day for its annual Memorial Day parade. After the morning parade, my Mom would organize an annual cookout in our backyard. The entire neighborhood was always invited. My Dad would spend hours cooking hamburgers and hotdogs for everyone. The afternoon would always conclude with a huge game of kickball with tons of neighborhood kids running around all over the place.

Holy Days and holidays are an essential part of allowing us to be fully human. Rest and fun are essential ingredients for a fully human life to develop and flourish.

For most people all of this sounds rather strange. My critics say that this is all "Leave it to Beaver" and "The Brady Bunch." I counter that by defending traditional family life and values against the prevailing culture which is out of control.

The founders of Magdalen College possessed the same values as my parents. They too understood the importance of the Sabbath and family life. For the first time in my life I was introduced to an all day celebration of a Catholic feast day. I learned then that something had been missing from my home parish. Holy Days consisted of Mass only. The ethnic celebrations so characteristic of Italian, Irish and Polish neighborhoods had vanished. John Meehan grew up in the Irish Catholic Boston of years gone by. He showed us how to celebrate a Catholic feast day and I am grateful for the memories of that experience. Community life is an integral part of Magdalen College and every holy day was celebrated with a special program of activities and delectable meals.

With the Legionaries of Christ, the concept of the Catholic feast day was taken to a whole other level. Mass was always celebrated with impeccable solemnity, lunch was ample and delicious, there were no classes and we spent a good part of the day playing basketball or soccer. We celebrated our Catholic Faith with intense joy. The experience of living in Spain, Italy and Mexico for many years was enriching, exciting and life changing.

As a pastor of a new parish in the city of Corpus Christi, I have taken these experiences, with the help of some very committed parishioners, and I have been able to develop a calendar of parish family events and celebrations.

The highlights of our parish family life calendar include the All Hallows Eve celebration organized by the Saint Helena Home Educators Association, the December 8th Marian Festival organized by our Spanish Mass community, the Christmas Midnight Mass Pot-luck dinner organized by our Filipino community, our Epiphany celebration organized by our CCD catechists, and our annual Pro-life 4th of July celebration. Recently we have added to these events a New Year's Eve jazz party which follows a 10:00 PM Mass, and a summer time cigar and wine tasting event accompanied by live jazz music. All of these events are very well attended by most of our parishioners and benefactors. Miguel Segovia, together with an enthusiastic group of volunteers, is constantly providing my parish with a wide assortment of excellent meals.

Most people are very hungry for community and I believe that it is essential that a parish provide parish family life. When I started St. Helena's I told the people that I did not give up a wife and kids of my own just for everyone to warm up a pew, drool and throw a dollar in the basket. Recently Al Hughes, one of my staff members, told me that he thinks that we have really begun to live out the spirit of the primitive Christian community. This is exactly the point.

Aside from our strong community moments, our Saint Helena 10 AM Mass community has a weekly Sunday brunch. Children enjoy the playground and while the adults enjoy each other's company. It is not uncommon for parishioners to still be at our Family Life Center until 1:00 PM. Meanwhile, our 12:15 PM Filipino Community has lunch together in the Family Life Center every Sunday. Our 6:00 PM Spanish Mass community enjoys frequent get-togethers throughout the year.

At Saint Helena's we also celebrate First Fridays as a parish family with the monthly First Friday Family Night.

Each parish is to be a living community of the Universal Church. Pope Benedict says that "the Church is Eucharistic fellowship". I find these words to be quite significant because they indicate that it is not enough just to go to Sunday Mass as a private spectator. Each parish is a community or communion of believers. As living members of the parish family, we are called not only to worship, but to participate in the community life of the parish. The parish is our church family.

"Faith is a personal act – the free response of the human person to the initiative of God who reveals himself. But faith is not an isolated act. No one can believe alone, just as no one can live alone. You have not given yourself faith as you have not given yourself life. The believer has received faith from others and should hand it on to others. Our love for Jesus and for our neighbor impels us to speak to others about our faith. Each believer is thus a link in a great chain of believers. I cannot believe without being carried by the faith of others, and by my faith I help support others in the faith" (Catechism of the Catholic Church, #166).

I firmly believe that after every Eucharistic Celebration, whenever possible, there should always be some kind of fellowship activity. Moreover, sprinkled throughout the liturgical year, there should be well-organized community activities that provide an opportunity for the entire parish to come together for fellowship.

John Meehan is the first to teach me the importance of Holy Week. During my years at the college it was customary for us to go home for Easter. But, after I graduated, Magdalen College developed a flawless celebration of the Sacred Triduum and most of the students remained on campus because there was nothing going on in their parishes back home.

My Holy Week experience in the seminary was certainly very beautiful and fulfilling. I have worked hard to implement all of these ideas and experiences in my parish. Our Holy Week liturgies are very well attended by devout parishioners.

Hillaire Belloc once wrote, "Wherever the Catholic sun doth shine, there's always laughter and good red wine. At least I've always found it so. Benedicamus Domino!" Adding to this thought, Father George Rutler said. "Joy on earth is a foretaste of the beatitude in heaven."

How then are we to live the Sabbath, the Lord's Day? There are two fundamental aspects to the Sabbath. First, we need to worship at our church, and secondly we must refrain from all unnecessary physical work.

Regarding the first practical aspect of the Sabbath, Sunday worship must be at the very center of our lives.

Pope John Paul II once wrote: "It is true that, in itself, the Sunday Eucharist is no different from the Eucharist celebrated on other days, nor can it be separated from liturgical and sacramental life as a whole. By its very nature, the Eucharist is an epiphany of the Church; and this is most powerfully expressed when the diocesan community gathers in prayer with its Pastor: The Church appears with special clarity when the holy People of God, all of them, are actively and fully sharing in the same liturgical celebrations — especially when it is the same Eucharist — sharing one prayer at one altar, at which the Bishop is presiding, surrounded by his presbyters and his ministers. This relationship with the Bishop and with the entire Church community is inherent in every Eucharistic celebration, even when the Bishop does not preside, regardless of the day of the week on which it is celebrated. The mention of the Bishop in the Eucharistic Prayer is the indication of this.

But because of its special solemnity and the obligatory presence of the community, and because it is celebrated on the day when Christ conquered death and gave us a share in his immortal life, the Sunday Eucharist expresses with greater emphasis its inherent ecclesial dimension. It becomes the paradigm for other Eucharistic celebrations. Each community, gathering all its members for the 'breaking of the bread', becomes the place where the mystery of the Church is concretely made present. In celebrating the Eucharist, the community opens itself to communion with the universal Church, imploring the Father to remember the Church throughout the world and make her grow in the unity of all the faithful with the Pope and with the Pastors of the particular Churches, until love is brought to perfection" (*Dies Domini*, #34).

We need to go to church every Sunday unless we are sick or the weather keeps us inside our homes. We need to dress appropriately for

Mass, because the church is God's house. We need to worship at Mass with full and conscious participation. Punctuality is a must.

The second aspect of our Sabbath is the prohibition from all unnecessary physical work. The Catechism of the Catholic Church states: "Just as God rested on the seventh day from all his work which he had done, human life has a rhythm of work and rest. The institution of the Lord's Day helps everyone enjoy adequate rest and leisure to cultivate their familial, cultural, social, and religious lives.

On Sundays and other holy days of obligation, the faithful are to refrain from engaging in work or activities that hinder the worship owed to God, the joy proper to the Lord's Day, the performance of the works of mercy, and the appropriate relaxation of mind and body. Family needs or important social service can legitimately excuse from the obligation of Sunday rest. The faithful should see to it that legitimate excuses do not lead to habits prejudicial to religion, family life, and health" (#2184, #2185).

This means that we are to do housework, yard work and shopping on other days, not on Sunday. Although it is true that some people will have to work because they are involved with service orientated professions (hospitals and restaurants), employers of these types of professions have a moral obligation to provide their employees time for worship and adequate rest.

Aside from the problems that secularism and materialism have caused in our culture, the bottom line is the fact that most of us simply just do not know how to rest. We are a very active people, and we need to recover the true sense of leisure.

Sunday rest is not simply watching sports all day on television with a couple of six packs of beer, nor is the solution eight hours of spiritual reading. We need to recapture the real meaning of leisure.

During my years in Spain and Mexico, it would be inevitable that interesting conversations with either Spaniards or Mexicans would take place regarding the differences between their countries and ours. One man put it bluntly: "Look, the difference between us and you is that we work in order to live, and you live in order to work." The root of America's extreme activity is a profound restlessness rooted in troubled consciences and lives that have lost the sense of what it means to be a creature of God. This frantic pace of life is being put to sleep with sex, drugs, alcohol, excessive entertainment and frantic work schedules. Most people equate true leisure to laziness and irresponsibility.

In ancient Athens, a man noticed the great storyteller Aesop playing childish games with some little boys. He laughed and jeered at Aesop, asking him why he wasted his time in such frivolous activity.

Aesop responded by picking up a bow, loosening its string, and placing it on the ground. Then he said to the critical Athenian, "Now, answer the riddle, if you can. Tell us what the unstrung bow implies."

The man looked at it for several moments but had no idea what point Aesop was trying to make. Aesop explained, "If you keep a bow always bent, it will break eventually; but if you let it go slack, it will be more fit for use when you want it."

Getting back to Catholic feast days for a moment, let us remember that Holy Days of Obligation should be considered just like a Sunday. For the most part, the Catholic Church in America has lost all sense of the Catholic feast day. I am creating a Catholic culture in my parish, but this is not an easy thing to do. However, more and more people are catching on to the importance of celebrating our holy days.

As our country becomes more and more secularized and materialistic we will have to live our feast days counter-culture. You can start by taking the day off. If your parish does not have anything going on for the holy day, start something. If no one is interested, start a small home based Catholic community with like minded Catholics.

During one of my recent summer visits to my parents' home who now live in Binghamton, NY, we were all playing a favorite card game on the back patio one Sunday afternoon. All of a sudden a neighbor began to mow his lawn with a very loud lawnmower. The noise of the lawnmower pierced the silence of the Sabbath. Modern man needs long moments of silence. Modern man needs a day without machines and gadgets.

"To avoid silence, we blindly grasp diversion, distraction. As an effect of all this, disintegration is produced within us. This ends up by giving birth to the feeling of aloneness, alienation, sadness and anxiety. This is the tragedy of the people of our day. Without a doubt, the periodic cultivation of silence, solitude and contemplation are more necessary, religiously and psychologically, than ever before. Our interiority is assaulted and battered by speed, noise and frenzy; we are at the same time, our own victim and executioner; and we end up feeling insecure and unhappy" (Ignacio Larrañaga, Sensing Your Hidden Presence, p. 187).

During the year, national holidays not only provide another moment of rest, they also provide an opportunity to remind ourselves who we are as a nation. It is unfortunate that so many businesses remain open even on national holidays. A country that does not enjoy true leisure will become fragmented and isolated.

I have had the blessing to live in Spain for five years and Mexico for six years. After my ordination to the priesthood I have been able to return to Spain, but living in Texas has given me the opportunity to spend numerous vacations in Mexico.

As soon as one arrives to Mexico the presence of children, young people and strong family life are apparent and striking. People actually smile. Although they live simply, they seem happy and content. Back at home, whenever I shop at Walmart, Sam's or a local supermarket, I am struck by the ever so apparent negativity, sadness, depression and obesity. Something is terribly wrong.

When a people no longer understand true leisure, they no longer know how to live. Do not get sucked into this matrix of despair.

I enjoy noticing what my parishioners do to develop true leisure in their lives and in their families. Here are just some examples.

Jaime is a very successful doctor from Venezuela. He enjoys travelling with his family every year at Christmas time and every summer. He accumulates mileage points gathered from the travels that he has to do for the many conferences that he delivers during the year. In this way, he is able to fly his entire family to beautiful places in Europe and throughout the United States.

Jorge, another very successful doctor from Guatemala enjoys working on his bonsai trees as a restful leisure activity. He runs almost every morning and frequently plays tennis with his friends. He also enjoys fine cigars. Jorge's wife is an accomplished artist. She finds rest in her beautiful work.

Jim and Lisa are very hard working people. They have a motor home which is parked in the lovely town of Rockport, Texas. During the summer they spend long weekends at their campsite.

Keith, a young computer programmer who now lives in Houston with his charming wife Amanda, loves to surf. He calls the beach area by the Bob Hall Pier on Padre Island, Texas his *sanctuary.*

Judith, a retired English teacher, finds solace and renewal by visiting her children and grandchildren.

Nury, a lively woman from Spain loves to travel with her American husband Larry. They visit with her family in Spain and in Argentina. While travelling to South America, Larry likes to go off on his own to explore indigenous archeological sites throughout the region.

Al and Jeannie travel each year to California to visit their daughters. Instead of taking a quick flight from Corpus Christi, they prefer to take the train from San Antonio. Al, a retired Air Force Colonel, loves trains and finds the trip restful and renewing.

Patti, Charles, Kevin and Amelia continually encourage their family to get together at Patti's mom's house for Sunday dinner and holidays. Marguerite Feudo, Patti's mom and Kevin's aunt, makes the most delicious homemade ravioli that her deceased husband Ron always enjoyed. After dinner, the stories about the Feudo grocery stores begin. These are always great stories. It is important that we tell our stories and pass them on to the next generation. Family stories keep the family together.

My own parents have an incredible sense of humor. Whenever we get together there are always plenty of stories to be retold which have already been passed on to my niece and my nephews.

One of my favorite stories took place when my Dad had left his small restaurant in order to manage a large truck stop restaurant in Binghamton, New York. He later became the manager of the entire chain of restaurants. When he first arrived, no one really knew his outspoken managerial style, but they quickly found it out.

One day in 1979 or 1980 he noticed his managers and staff nervously gathered together in front of a big bay window which looked out to the rather large parking area. He asked what the problem was and they explained that a small group of hippies were in the parking lot with their Volkswagen bus and they were setting up camp, right in the middle of the parking lot. The managers and the staff did not know what to do about the situation.

My Dad approached the window and slid it open and yelled out at the top of his voice, "Hey you! Get the hell out of here!" He then looked at his shocked employees and said, "That's how you handle that."

Suggested Reading

Dies Domini – John Paul II

The Bad Catholics Guide to Good Living – John Zmirak and Denise Mattchowiak

The Bad Catholics Guide to Wine, Whiskey and Song - John Zmirak and Denise Mattchowiak

Leisure: The Basis of Culture – Josef Pieper

In Tune with the Word: A Theory of Festivity – Josef Pieper

CHAPTER EIGHT

PUTTING IT ALL TOGETHER

Do not count on human leaders, institutions, organizations or even the culture to bring about the change in your life that you are longing for. You have to be responsible for your own life. You are the only one that can make the best decision of your life.

Authenticity, maturity and coherence *are* possible in a world filled with hypocrites, charlatans, false prophets and corrupt leaders.

There is an ancient Greek story which is attributed to Diogenes of Sinope. The story is about an old hermit that walked around the village day and night carrying a lit lantern. Even during the day the lantern remained lit. Curiously the villagers asked him why he was walking around with a lit lantern during the day. "I am searching for an honest man," was the hermit's immediate response.

This story from Greek mythology reminds us of the words from the Holy Bible: *"Wisdom calls aloud in the streets, she raises her voice in the public squares; she calls out at the street corners, she delivers her message at the city gates, 'You ignorant people, how much longer will you cling to your ignorance? How much longer will mockers revel in their mocking and hold knowledge contemptible?'"* (Proverbs 1: 20-22).

Live your life before God. One day we will all stand before God and give him an accounting of the way we have lived the gift of life. When we die, we will stand alone before God.

Fidelity is an austere virtue. Fidelity demands self-knowledge, generosity, sacrifice and a lot of courage. The daily struggle and the failures can be overwhelming at times. Fidelity is an adventure, and the *"good fight"* is exhilarating.

As time goes on, we can become weary of the battle. Personally, I believe it is far better to drag an exhausted body and spirit through the difficulties of life, rather than to give in to the promptings of the flesh which make us yearn for an easier, self-indulgent life. Rather than to give in to the sirens of comfort, I prefer to hear these words from my Lord at the moment of death: *"I know too that you have perseverance, and have suffered for my name without growing tired"* (Revelation 2: 3).

STEP ONE – THE JOURNEY OF SELF KNOWLEDGE

Begin your journey to the new you by understanding who you are as a Catholic. You are a layperson. This means that you are not a priest, a deacon, a nun, or a brother. This means that you are not supposed to be walking around with robes on all the time or rosary beads hanging from your eyeballs.

As a card carrying member of the rank and file of the Catholic Church you are called, through the Sacrament of Baptism, to be holy; to be an active member of the Catholic Church; and to sanctify the temporal order by the witness of your life and your apostolic activity. Living the life to which you are called, requires discipline. It is time to get your butt into gear.

STEP TWO – PERSONAL DISCIPLINE

You are very busy and life is very demanding. Time passes by quickly. It is crucial that you acquire personal discipline by organizing your life. Discipline is essential if you are going to live out the spiritual life that will make you happy and get you into heaven.

The only way that you can have a serious and intimate friendship with God is through the discipline of a realistic schedule of your time, duties and activities.

"You dopes need a schedule. You lazy slobs need to form your will. Stop fiddilin' and didilin' and do something with your lives. It is time to stop picking your nose and get your butt into gear."

STEP THREE – DEVELOP A SPIRITUAL LIFE

Remember that the struggle with sin is not going to be an easy enterprise in this crazy and dysfunctional world. Due to the effects of Original Sin, an inner force will always push you in the wrong direction. Continual effort is necessary to direct the inner movement of your ego and allow the presence of grace to take control of your thoughts, desires and actions.

If the spiritual life is a constant struggle because of original sin, then the present circumstances of contemporary culture make this struggle even more difficult. We have all grown up in a culture that denies nothing. Our decadent world is attractive to fallen human nature. It is easy to succumb to any of the seven deadly sins of pride, avarice, envy, wrath, lust, gluttony and sloth.

Without a doubt, authentic Christianity is difficult to live and demands radical decisions on our part. We must never be afraid of the struggle.

Although developing and strengthening your spiritual life requires an intense effort on your part, all your hard work will only be successful with the help of God's grace. A daily disciplined regimen of prayer, scripture reading and sacramental life helps to develop those channels of grace through which the Holy Spirit gives you the ability to control yourself and conquer your baser tendencies.

Prayer is not God's Coke Machine for the human race. No! Prayer is a continual being in love with the awesome God of unconditional love. Faith allows us to pray. Faith is the greatest gift that God gives to each of us. Faith allows us to acquire an intimate communion with God which can become more intimate than the conjugal love of married spouses.

It is essential that you incorporate within your busy day a well organized prayer life and stick to your plan.

How do you expect to be happy in this life and make it to heaven without a serious prayer life?

STEP FOUR – MAKE A CONSCIOUS DECISION TO CHANGE

Are laziness, apathy and complacency keeping you from living the kind of life God intended you to live from all eternity? If your answer is yes, then make a life changing decision right now to change your life forever.

The Eucharist, the Scriptures, the Rosary, quiet meditation and the frequent use of the Sacrament of Confession are the tools that God has given you to get to heaven.

We do live in a very challenging world. It is not easy to be a serious Catholic. Now more than ever the Catholic Church and the world need heroes. Saints are heroes.

Everything that I have spoken to you about in this book has been made possible by one historical event that changed the world forever. That singular event was the birth of Jesus Christ in Bethlehem.

I am sure that most of you have seen the movie "It's a Wonderful Life." James Stewart stars in this Frank Capra classic as George Bailey, an average American businessman who lives in a small, upstate New York town.

Bailey's Uncle Billy, who assists his nephew with a struggling savings and loan bank, misplaces $8,000, thus catapulting Bailey into a terrible crisis. The money cannot be found because Mr. Potter, played by Lionel Barrymore, has discovered the money and kept it. George Bailey becomes totally discouraged and considers ending his life before he defaults on his creditors and ends up in jail.

Clarence, George Bailey's guardian angel, comes to the rescue. He tells George that he has been granted a wonderful gift, the ability to walk through his life as if he had not been born. During the rest of the movie, Clarence is able to show George what a wonderful life he has had and how much of an effect he has had on the people of his small town; moreover, what their lives would have been like had he not been born.

What would our lives be like if Jesus had not been born? We need to open our minds and our hearts and allow this Savior to transform our lives.

In 1944, Louis Jordan, a very popular jazz and blues musician, songwriter and bandleader produced a song that later became very famous. "Is You Is or Is You Ain't My Baby" has been sung by such great artists like Bing Crosby, Nat "King" Cole, the Andrew Sisters, Dinah Washington, B.B.

King and even contemporary artists like Diana Krall.

We live in an age where most people are not listening, doing their own thing and spoiled rotten. The Catholic Church and the world need a huge dose of real, mature, authentic and coherent Christianity. Is you is or is you ain't? No one can say that they can't live a serious Catholic life.

As I look back at my four years at Magdalen College, there is no doubt in my mind that those years were a gift from God. Through this book I have attempted, in a practical way, to pass on to you my own personal experience and how it shaped my life. In fact, I have spent my entire life after Magdalen College trying to pass this experience on to others. Many have listened, and some just do not seem interested. I have attempted to lessen my frustration by writing this book for you.

John Meehan has been one of my best friends. When I graduated in May of 1978, his parting words to me were these: "Wherever you are ordained and whenever you are ordained, I will be there". With the excitement of an intense seminary preparation, I had forgotten those words. However, nine and a half years later when I arrived to Rome for my ordination, Meehan's son, Father Kevin, also a member of the Legionaries of Christ, told me that his parents and his sister were coming over for my ordination.

Throughout all of these years since my graduation, John and I have maintained a very close relationship and we usually talk on the phone at least once a month.

One day a little more than a year ago, I decided to give John a call one Monday afternoon and I asked him how he was doing. "Everything is fine, except that I have cancer", was his response. I paused for a moment and then I said, "I know what you are going to do. You are going to sit out on your back porch and continue to smoke cigarettes and drink whisky". "You got that right", he affirmed. Then we both busted up laughing.

After exchanging one hilarious joke after another, I concluded our conversation by asking John if he still had the pine coffin in his basement that a friend had made for him years ago so that he could "contemplate eternity". "I sure do", Meehan asserted. "Good", I said. "Tonight you should take your pillow and blanket and give it a try." We both roared laughing.

Our conversation took place on a Monday afternoon. Monday is my *vegetable day* (my way of describing a day off). When I finished talking to

Meehan, I drove over to Jim's house for our usual Monday evening get together.

As I was driving, the laughter subsided and the tears began to flow. Although our hope is in eternity, human loss is always difficult to deal with.

The following summer I made sure to visit the Meehan's when I went up to see my parents in Binghamton, New York. During our brief visit, Fr. Paul Sullivan from the Archdiocese of Boston and Tom Prendergast, both alumni from the college, joined us for dinner at the Meehan's home just outside of Concord, New Hampshire.

Tom brought along his guitar and the three Irishmen sang Irish ballads for at least two hours. Years ago when Tom was a student at the college, these ballads were always a popular part of any social event at Magdalen College.

I did not know any of the lyrics, so I intervened with some corny jokes and we had a great time. Of course there was plenty of whisky and great cigars.

While they were singing, I sat back and thought to myself: here is a man who is dying from cancer. A radical is sitting in the White House. The college that Meehan ran for so many years is going through a terrible identity crisis and the religious order that I was a part of and Meehan's sons Kevin and Timothy are still a part of is falling apart. Yet, here we are, singing, laughing and telling jokes.

And why could we do that?

Because our hope is not in people. People are limited. Our hope is not in institutions and programs. Our hope is not in countries. Nations rise and fall. Our hope is in Jesus Christ. And we can place all of our hope in Jesus Christ because "he is the same yesterday, today and tomorrow" (Hebrews 13: 8). We are first and foremost citizens of a kingdom that is not of this world.

Congratulations, you have succeeded in entering the "no whine zone." When you become discouraged from time to time, and you will, re-read this last chapter and renew your commitment to Christ. Be sure to recall your small successes in becoming a more viable citizen of his kingdom. Pray harder; laugh more; and love more abundantly.

Always be assured of my daily prayers and support for everyone who reads this book.

AN EPILOGUE

by

Jennifer Hartline

There are days when I do battle with a deadly heart disease. It comes in two forms, both rather sneaky in how they creep up on me and worm their way into my heart. They are cynicism and indifference. It's not so much that I choose them; it's that I make no effort to refuse them.

Clearly, many of us are suffering this malady. This is the disease that zaps our energy and steals our excitement. It leaves us weary and lazy and full of handy excuses. It eats away at devotion and leaves our souls empty. Christendom in America is deeply infected with this life-sapping sickness. It is why so many Christians have been enticed and beguiled by power and popularity and persuaded to compromise. Without passion, without zeal, without fervor, we are lifeless and faith is so easily cast aside.

St. Augustine prescribes the cure: We need a new romance. *"To fall in love with God is the greatest of romances, to seek him the greatest adventure, to find him the greatest human achievement."* What the cynical and indifferent heart needs is a healthy dose of romance.

We have every reason to be enthralled in romance! The greatest gesture of love known to the universe was made toward each of us by the Author of True Love. We are not simply liked and enjoyed; we are passionately, deeply, obsessively loved!

How does it go again?

"God so understood the world…"

"God so cared for the world…"

"God so respected the world…"

"God so accepted the world…"

"God so disdained the world…"

"God so rejected the world…"

No…God so LOVED the world that he gave his only begotten Son, that whosoever believes in Him will not perish but have everlasting life. God made a bold and unflinching proclamation of abiding, endless love to all mankind, and Jesus came to be made a fool of, all in the hope that He would win the hearts of His beloved ones. Only a passionate lover is willing to look foolish for his beloved.

People, we desperately need a new romance. We need to take a good, long look with fresh eyes at the Lover of our souls and internalize the high price he paid for the chance to be reunited with us. I hope we have not stared at our painted images of God for so long that we are no longer impressed by what we see, for it's not the typical picture of enchantment. Unadulterated passion and pure, ambitious love are not presented to us in flowers and sunsets, but in straw, wood, nails and blood.

I wonder in our day if we can even comprehend the nature of real love. Do we spend much time anymore contemplating a love that isn't sexual or pleasure-oriented? Are we even inclined to pursue an endeavor that demands self-sacrifice?

"There will be terrible times in the last days. People will be lovers of themselves, lovers of money, boastful, proud, abusive, disobedient to their parents, ungrateful, unholy, without love, unforgiving, slanderous, without self-control, brutal, not lovers of the good, treacherous, rash, conceited, lovers of pleasure rather than lovers of God – having a form of godliness but denying its power. Have nothing to do with them" (2 Timothy 3:1-5).

We have lost the fervor of our affection for God because we have become deadened to the meaning of real love. Love gives. Love is not self-seeking. Love cannot keep anything for itself. This kind of love is increasingly foreign to us. Like some kind of Dead Sea that only receives and never gives of itself to anyone else, we die inside because we don't love. We must make a concerted effort to dwell on this crazy, extravagant love of God until it captures us again in the flush of romance. We need to fall in love with Jesus. It is the only cure for the cynical and indifferent heart.

We need that love to make us fearless in our devotion. We need the kind of passion that turns us into willing fools, people who couldn't care less what the world thinks of us. I want the kind of passion and love for Christ that is oblivious to everything but him. If he holds my heart, I need nothing else. The sound of his voice makes my heart pound, and there's no room in my ears for any scorn or insult. I say I want this kind of passion and love because I'm not quite there yet. But I'm being wooed, and the more I attend to his affection, the more this romance grows, and the more my heart longs only for Jesus. I want the love described in the Song of Solomon: *"Place me like a seal over your heart, like a seal on your arm; for love is as strong as death, its jealousy unyielding as the grave. It burns like blazing fire, like a mighty flame. Many waters cannot quench love; rivers cannot wash it away."*

This is the love that turns ordinary people into saints! This is the love that turns you and me into the hands and feet of Jesus in the world. This is the love that softens the most hardened of hearts, the love the world simply cannot ignore. It is this love that gives us courage and compels us to be faithful no matter the cost.

The heart in love with Jesus has no room for compromise or deception, since it only desires more of Jesus. The moral courage and conviction we lack, the absence of zeal and fervor in our faith is easily cured, if we will purposely incline ourselves toward him. It is a sweet romance that beckons to us…let us fall in love again!

ACKNOWLEDGEMENTS

This project began with a pad of yellow paper and a pen looking over the Pacific Ocean. Over the course of one year, the manuscript of this book began to organically develop as many friends graciously read it and provided me with many excellent suggestions and corrections. I am very grateful for their time and the encouragement that they provided me. I would especially like to thank Matt Abbott, Judith Barnett, Judie Brown, Michael Brown, Linda Concert, Rose DeCovolo, Deacon Keith Fournier, Jennifer Hartline, Albert Hughes, Alison Jones, Ken Justice, Angie Gilbert, Steve Guilding, Father Sam Medley, SOLT, John Meehan, Jorge Mendizabal, Virginia Metz, Meagan Montez, Donna-Marie Cooper O'Boyle, Steve Pokorny, Ray Reeves and Stephen Vanderlaske.

Special thanks go to James Hickel who read and re-read the different versions of my manuscript as it developed. I am very grateful for his encouragement and advice during this project.

I would also like to thank Ada Segovia for her secretarial assistance and for Lisa Hickel, my always faithful and diligent parish secretary who handles so many details of daily parish life. Her dedication allowed me to bury myself in my office and finish this project. Thanks also go to James Ficarro and Kateri Reyes for taking care of the Internet marketing of my books. Special thanks go to Patricia Salinas of Kingsville, Texas who handles the distribution of my books. Also, I would like to thank the talented Ligia Mendizabal who once again did the cover design.

Finally, I would like to thank *"Mexico, querido y lindo."* The beautiful people and locations of this great country provided me incredible opportunities to listen to God and to write. Muchas gracias por todo.

ABOUT THE AUTHOR

Father James Farfaglia was born on February 20, 1956 to Salvatore and Eleanor Farfaglia, in Stamford, Connecticut. Father is the oldest of four children. His sister Donna lives in Phoenix, Arizona, his brother John lives in Saratoga Springs, New York and his youngest sister Amy is a member of a religious order.

When Father was five, Sal and Ellie took their young family to the beautiful New England town of Ridgefield, Connecticut. Ridgefield is where Father James grew up. He went to Saint Mary's Catholic elementary school and then graduated from Ridgefield High School in 1974. He spent all of his Saturdays and summers of his boyhood working alongside his Dad at the family restaurant in Pound Ridge, New York, just across the Connecticut – New York border.

During the tumultuous years of 1968 – 1974, Father developed a deep passion for politics. Although he loved serving Mass as an altar boy, he never experienced a desire to become a priest. His mind was set on becoming a lawyer and he wanted to run for public office. When he was a freshman in high school, he founded and chaired a chapter of the Young Americans for Freedom.

God's divine providence led the high school graduate to a new Catholic College that was just beginning in New Hampshire. Magdalen College welcomed their first group of students in September, 1974 and it is there where Father James met Jim Hickel from Anchorage, Alaska. They were roommates for four years and became lifelong friends. During his sophomore year at Magdalen College, Father experienced a profound calling which led him to the Catholic priesthood.

Upon graduating college in 1978, Father joined the Legionaries of Christ. At that time, the Legion of Christ was just beginning to develop in the United States and Father had many opportunities to help in the growth of the congregation.

His path to the Roman Catholic priesthood brought him to study in Spain and Rome. Throughout his years with the Legionaries of Christ, he founded and developed seminaries, schools and the Regnum Christi lay movement in Spain, Mexico, Canada and throughout different parts of the United States.

Once again, divine providence was at work and God led him to parish life in May, 1999. He met Bishop Edmond Carmody who was then the Bishop of Tyler, Texas. Bishop Carmody asked Father to found and build a new parish in Lufkin, Texas. Saint Andrew the Apostle Catholic Church was built in 6 months and the rectory within 3 months.

When the project was completed, God's providence was at work again and Bishop Carmody was transferred to the Corpus Christi diocese in March, 2000. Although the founding of Saint Andrew's was a very rewarding ministry, through much prayer and discernment, Father decided to follow Bishop Carmody to South Texas. Bishop Carmody welcomed him at the end of March, 2001 with open arms and put him to work with Msgr. Michael Heras.

Both Msgr. Heras and Father James became instant friends. During his time as parochial vicar of Our Lady of Perpetual Help Catholic Church, Father assisted Msgr. Heras in the growth and development of the parish. Father co-founded with Msgr. Heras the Lay Formation Program and they both took on the exciting, but rather challenging project of co-founding a new parish, Saint Helena of the True Cross of Jesus. Saint Helena's was elevated to a parish on March 17, 2004 by Bishop Carmody, where Father James currently serves as the pastor. He is a diocesan priest for the Diocese of Corpus Christi.

Aside from his duties at Saint Helena's, Father has his own Internet ministry. His weekly Internet homily, both in the written form and in the audio podcast form, has become very popular. He manages his own blog, *Illegitimi non carborundum,* which is a no-nonsense, hard-hitting commentary on current events. His homilies and articles frequently appear on Catholic Online, Spirit Daily and Matt Abbott's Renew America column.

Father's first book, <u>*Man to Man: A Real Priest, Speaks to Real Men about Marriage, Sexuality and Family Life*</u> has become a very popular resource for men who want to live a faithful and joy filled marriage. He has been the guest on numerous well-known Catholic radio stations around the country where has spoken about his book.

Father is militantly involved in the pro-life movement. Since January, 2007, he has been leading a crusade to close down the only remaining abortion clinic in the city of Corpus Christi. He is a member of the board of directors of Hope House, a

Corpus Christi home for unwed mothers, a position that he holds close to his pastoral heart. Father also assists Human Life International as a member of their board of directors.

Father's parish founded their own Knights of Columbus council and Father James is an active member.

Aside from his demanding duties as a Catholic priest, Father loves movies, he is an avid Three Stooges fan, enjoys swimming, basketball, soccer and the outdoors. He listens to jazz and he is a passionate *cigar aficionado*. You can contact Father at fjficthus@gmail.com and you can visit him on the web at www.FatherJames.org.